www.wadsworth.com

wadsworth.com is the World Wide Web site for Wadsworth and is your direct source to dozens of online resources.

At *wadsworth.com* you can find out about supplements, demonstration software, and student resources. You can also send email to many of our authors and preview new publications and exciting new technologies.

wadsworth.com
Changing the way the world learns®

CALIFORNIA POLITICS AND GOVERNMENT

A Practical Approach

Seventh Edition

Larry N. Gerston
San Jose State University

Terry Christensen
San Jose State University

THOMSON
™
WADSWORTH

Australia • Canada • Mexico • Singapore • Spain
United Kingdom • United States

Publisher, Political Science: Clark Baxter

Executive Editor, Political Science: David Tatom

Senior Developmental Editor: Stacey Sims

Assistant Editor: Heather Hogan

Editorial Assistant: Dianna Long

Technology Project Manager: Melinda Newfarmer

Marketing Manager: Janise Fry

Associate Project Manager, Editorial Production:
Emily Smith

Print/Media Buyer: Jessica Reed

Permissions Editor: Kiely Sexton

Production Service: Graphic World Publishing Services

Illustrator: Graphic World Illustration Studio

Cover Designer: Jeanette Barber

Cover Image: AP/Wide World Photos

Compositor: Graphic World Inc.

Text and Cover Printer: Webcom

For more information about our products,
contact us at:
**Thomson Learning Academic Resource
Center
1-800-423-0563**

For permission to use material from this text,
contact us by:
Phone: 1-800-730-2214
Fax: 1-800-730-2215
Web: http://www.thomsonrights.com

Library of Congress Control Number: 2002114677

ISBN 0-534-61740-9

Wadsworth/Thomson Learning
10 Davis Drive
Belmont, CA 94002-3098
USA

Asia
Thomson Learning
5 Shenton Way #01-01
UIC Building
Singapore 068808

Australia
Nelson Thomson Learning
102 Dodds Street
South Melbourne, Victoria 3205
Australia

Canada
Nelson Thomson Learning
1120 Birchmount Road
Toronto, Ontario M1K 5G4
Canada

Europe/Middle East/Africa
Thomson Learning
High Holborn House
50/51 Bedford Row
London WC1R 4LR
United Kingdom

Latin America
Thomson Learning
Seneca, 53
Colonia Polanco
11560 Mexico D.F.
Mexico

Spain
Paraninfo Thomson Learning
Calle/Magallanes, 25
28015 Madrid, Spain

To
the futures of
Adam David, Lee Daniel, and
Rachel Sarah Gerston

and

the memories of
Anna and Teter Christensen and
Tillie and Chester Welliever

ABOUT THE AUTHORS

Larry N. Gerston, professor of political science at San Jose State University, attempts to blend politics and theory whenever possible, viewing both as key components of the political process. He has worked for a Los Angeles County supervisor and a California assembly member. Professor Gerston has written *Making Public Policy: From Conflict to Resolution* (1983), *American Government: Politics, Process, and Policies* (1993), *Public Policy Making: Process and Principles* (1997), and *Public Policymaking in a Democratic Society: A Guide to Civic Engagement* (2002). He has co-authored *Politics in the Golden State* (1984, 1988, with Terry Christensen) and *The Deregulated Society* (1988, with Cynthia Fraleigh and Robert Schwab). Professor Gerston writes a monthly column on politics for *San Jose Magazine* and has served since 1980 as the political analyst for television station NBC11 in San Jose. Between elections and other political adventures, he enjoys his wife, Elisa, and their three children, Adam, Lee, and Rachel.

Terry Christensen, professor of political science at San Jose State University, teaches and writes on California state and local politics and British politics. He has authored *Neighborhood Survival* (1979), a book about urban renewal in London; *Movers and Shakers* (1982, with Philip J. Trounstine), a study of community power; *Reel Politics* (1987), an analysis of American political movies; and *Local Politics: Governing at the Grassroots* (1995). A longtime political activist, Christensen has worked with a wide variety of community organizations and political campaigns and has served as a delegate to the South Bay AFL-CIO Labor Council and as a member of the Democratic State Central Committee. As his history may suggest, he advocates learning by participant observation, and he helped develop San Jose State's extensive internship program. He was selected San Jose State University's Outstanding Professor for 1997–1998.

PREFACE

California Politics and Government is designed as a brief introduction for observers, participants, and first-time students of California politics. We have attempted to cover the topic in a readable fashion, balancing the basics of state politics and government with analysis, color, and brevity. As with earlier editions, we emphasize California's political institutions and processes. The state's historical evolution dominates our first chapter. Succeeding chapters on political institutions include their historical development as well as their current operations. Cultural diversity is another theme that runs through every chapter. We have included the nuts and bolts of the political process and institutions, along with frequent references to the people, groups, and issues that move them. Most of all, we have tried to make sense out of the maze of contradictions known as California.

In earlier editions of this book, we noted the rapidity of change in California and its politics. Yet, as we complete work on the seventh edition, we continue to marvel at change as one of the few constants in California. Some of the changes involve elections and term limits, including those from the 2002 election, which are discussed throughout the book. Other changes stem from the state's economy, which thrived at the beginning of the new millennium but is now in recession, resulting in a huge budget deficit and a crisis in state services. The budget crisis has been exacerbated by the energy crisis of 2001 and the "war on terrorism." All of these and other recent events are discussed in this new edition.

As in the previous edition, we have integrated discussion of public policy issues and political institutions, rather than including a separate chapter on public policy. We did this to shorten and tighten the book, but we also believe this clarifies the relationship between politics, political institutions, and public policy outcomes. We have also continued our expansion of the chapter on state–federal relations, as the composition of the state's congressional delegation changes and issues such as immigration, affirmative action, the environment, and federal spending continue to attract attention. Included in this chapter is a timely discussion of the impact of the national war on terrorism on California.

We have also updated and expanded two sections at the end of each chapter. "Learn More on the World Wide Web" provides students and instructors with useful Web sites pertinent to the topics of each chapter, and "Learn More at the Library" refers readers to some of our own favorite books on the topics. As previously, key terms, institutions, and events appear in bold throughout the book. These terms are briefly defined in the glossary at the back of our book to provide a quick reference source for students.

Many friends and colleagues helped us develop and produce this book. Adam Gerston, Wendy Chang, and Jason Yee provided timely and intrepid research assistance. Elisa Gerston provided valuable in-house editing, for which the bleary-eyed authors are grateful. Public workers in the governor's office, the legislature, the courts, and elsewhere helped us in our search for the most up-to-date data. Colleagues at San Jose State University and elsewhere offered suggestions which we followed and appreciated (send more!). We continue to learn from our students and our many friends in politics, journalism, and academia.

We're grateful to the production staff at Thomson/Wadsworth who worked on an unusually tight schedule. They include David Tatom, executive editor, political science; Stacey Sims, senior developmental editor; Emily Smith, associate project editor, editorial production; Janise Fry, marketing manager; and Suzanne Kastner, production manager. To these and many others, we offer our deepest thanks.

Larry N. Gerston

Terry Christensen

CONTENTS

CHAPTER 1

CALIFORNIA'S PEOPLE, ECONOMY, AND POLITICS: YESTERDAY, TODAY, AND TOMORROW   1

Colonization, Rebellion, and Statehood   1
Railroads, Machines, and Reform   3
The Great Depression and World War II   5
Postwar Politics   7
California Today   8
Into the Future   13
Notes   14
Learn More on the World Wide Web   14
Learn More at the Library   14

CHAPTER 2

POLITICAL PARTIES AND DIRECT DEMOCRACY: TOO MUCH DEMOCRACY?   15

The Progressive Legacy   15
Party Organization–Structure and Supporters   17
Direct Democracy   21
The Politics of Ballot Propositions   23
Political Parties, Direct Democracy, and California Politics   25
Notes   26
Learn More on the World Wide Web   26
Learn More at the Library   26

CHAPTER 3

**VOTERS, CANDIDATES, CAMPAIGNS, AND THE MEDIA:
THE MIX OF MONEY AND MARKETING 27**

The Voters 27
The Candidates 28
Campaigning California Style 30
The Media in California Politics 35
Elections, Campaigns, and the Media 38
Notes 38
Learn More on the World Wide Web 39
Learn More at the Library 39

CHAPTER 4

INTEREST GROUPS: THE POWER BEHIND THE DOME 40

The Evolution of Group Power in California 40
The Groups 41
Techniques and Targets: Interest Groups at Work 45
Regulating Groups 49
Measuring Group Clout: Money, Numbers, and Credibility 50
Notes 50
Learn More on the World Wide Web 51
Learn More at the Library 51

CHAPTER 5

THE LEGISLATURE: THE PERILS OF POLICYMAKING 52

The Making and Unmaking of a Model Legislature 52
How a Bill Becomes a Law 59
Unfinished Business 64
Notes 64
Learn More on the World Wide Web 65
Learn More at the Library 65

CHAPTER 6

COURTS, JUDGES, AND POLITICS: CALIFORNIA LAW   66

The California Court System   66
The Courts at Work   70
The High Court as a Political Battleground   73
Governors, Voters, and the Courts   74
Courts and the Politics of Crime   77
Politics and the Courts   78
Notes   78
Learn More on the World Wide Web   79
Learn More at the Library   79

CHAPTER 7

THE EXECUTIVE BRANCH: COPING WITH FRAGMENTED AUTHORITY   80

The Governor: First among Equals   80
The Supporting Cast   87
The Bureaucracy   91
Making the Pieces Fit   92
Notes   92
Learn More on the World Wide Web   93
Learn More at the Library   93

CHAPTER 8

TAXING AND SPENDING: BUDGETARY POLITICS AND POLICIES   94

The Budgetary Process   94
Revenue Sources   97
Spending   101
Modern State Budgets: Too Little, Too Much, or Just Right?   105
Notes   106
Learn More on the World Wide Web   106
Learn More at the Library   106

CHAPTER 9

LOCAL GOVERNMENT: POLITICS AT THE GRASSROOTS 107

Counties and Cities 107
Power in the City: Council Members, Managers, and Mayors 111
More Governments 113
Direct Democracy in Local Politics 116
Land Use: Coping with Growth 117
Taxing and Spending 118
Local Limits 120
Notes 120
Learn More on the World Wide Web 121
Learn More at the Library 121

CHAPTER 10

STATE–FEDERAL RELATIONS: CONFLICT, COOPERATION, AND CHAOS 122

California's Clout in Washington 123
Terrorism 124
Immigration 125
Affirmative Action and Discrimination 127
Air Pollution 127
Water 129
Shared Resources 130
Changed Rules, New Directions 131
Notes 132
Learn More on the World Wide Web 133
Learn More at the Library 133

Glossary 135
Index 141

CHAPTER 1

CALIFORNIA'S PEOPLE, ECONOMY, AND POLITICS: YESTERDAY, TODAY, AND TOMORROW

Like so much else about California, our state's politics appears to change constantly, unpredictably, and even inexplicably. Politicians seem to rise and fall more because of their personalities and campaign treasuries than because of their policies or political party ties. The governor and the legislature appear to be competing with one another rather than solving our problems. Multibillion-dollar campaigns ask voters to make decisions about issues that seem to emerge from nowhere only to see their decisions overturned by the courts. No wonder some Californians are confused or disillusioned about politics and disdain political participation. But however unpredictable or even disgusting California politics may appear, it is serious business that affects us all. And despite its volatility, California can be understood by examining its history and its present characteristics, especially its changing population and economy. Wave after wave of immigrants has made California a diverse, multicultural society, and new technologies repeatedly transform the state's economy. The resulting disparate ethnic and economic interests compete for the benefits and protections conferred by government and thus shape the state's politics. But to understand California today—and tomorrow— we need to know a little about its past and about the development of these competing interests.

COLONIZATION, REBELLION, AND STATEHOOD

The first Californians were probably immigrants like the rest of us. Archaeologists believe that the ancestors of American Indians crossed over from Asia to Alaska thousands of years ago and then headed south.

By 1769 about 300,000 Native Americans were living mostly near the coast of what is now California when the Spaniards colonized the area with missions and military outposts.

These native Californians were brought to the missions as Catholic converts and workers, but European diseases and the destruction of their culture reduced their numbers to about 100,000 by 1849. Disease and massacres wiped out entire tribes, and the Indian population continued to diminish through the nineteenth century. Today, less than 1 percent of California's population is Native American. Many feel deeply alienated from a society that has overwhelmed their peoples and cultures, and some strive mightily to preserve their traditions.

Apart from building missions, the Spaniards did little to develop their faraway possession, and little changed when Mexico, which included California within its boundaries, declared its independence from Spain in 1822. A few thousand Mexicans quietly raised cattle on vast ranches.

Meanwhile, expansionist interests in the United States cast covetous eyes on California's rich lands and access to the Pacific Ocean. When Mexico and the United States went to war over Texas in 1846, recent Yankee immigrants to California seized the moment and declared independence from Mexico. After the U.S. victory in Texas, Mexico surrendered its claim to possessions extending from Texas to California.

At about the same time, gold was discovered in California. The gold rush that followed increased the area's foreign population from 9,000 in 1846 to 264,000 in 1852. Many immigrants came directly from Europe. The first Chinese also arrived to work in the mines that yielded more than a billion dollars' worth of gold in five years.

The surge in population and commerce moved the new Californians to political action. By 1849 they had drafted a constitution, mostly copied from those of existing states, and requested statehood, which the U.S. Congress was only too glad to grant. The organization of the new state was remarkably similar to what we have today. The forty-eight delegates to the constitutional convention (only seven of whom were native-born Californians) set up a two-house legislature, a supreme court, and an executive branch consisting of a governor, a lieutenant governor, a controller, an attorney general, and a superintendent of public instruction. A bill of rights was also included in the constitution, but only white males were allowed to vote. The rights of women and racial minorities were ignored, and in addition to being denied the right to vote, California's Chinese, African American, and Native American residents were soon prohibited by law from owning land, testifying in court, or attending public schools.

As the gold rush ended, a land rush began. Unlike the land in other states, where small homesteads predominated, much of California's land had been concentrated in huge parcels created by Spanish and Mexican land grants. As early as 1870 a few hundred men owned most of the farmland. Their ranches were the forerunners of contemporary agribusiness corporations, and as the mainstay of the state's economy, they exercised even more clout than their modern successors.

In less than fifty years California had belonged to three different nations. During the same period, its economy had changed dramatically as hundreds of thousands of immigrants from all over the world came to claim their share of the "Golden State." The pattern of a rapidly evolving, multicultural polity had been set.

RAILROADS, MACHINES, AND REFORM

Technology wrought the next transformation in the form of railroads. In 1861 Sacramento merchants Charles Crocker, Mark Hopkins, Collis Huntington, and Leland Stanford founded the railroad that would become the **Southern Pacific.** Then they persuaded Congress to provide millions of dollars in land grants and loan subsidies for a railroad to link California with the eastern United States, thus greatly expanding the market for California products. Leland Stanford, then governor, used his influence to provide state assistance. Cities and counties also contributed, under threat of being bypassed by the railroad. To obtain workers at cheap rates, the railroad builders imported 15,000 Chinese laborers.

When the transcontinental track was completed in 1869, the Southern Pacific expanded its system throughout the state by building new lines and buying up others. The railroad crushed competitors by cutting its shipping charges, and by the 1880s it had become the state's dominant transportation company as well as its largest private landowner, owning 11 percent of the entire state. With its business agents doubling as political representatives in almost every California city and county, the Southern Pacific soon developed a formidable political machine. "The Octopus," as novelist Frank Norris called the railroad, worked through both the Republican and Democratic political parties to place allies in state and local offices. Once there, they were obliged to protect the interests of the Southern Pacific if they wanted to continue in office. County tax assessors supported by the machine set favorable tax rates for the railroad while the machine-controlled legislature ensured a hands-off policy by state government.

THE WORKINGMEN'S PARTY

People in small towns and rural areas who were unwilling to support the machine lost jobs, business, and other benefits. Some moved to cities (especially San Francisco, where manufacturing jobs were increasingly available). Many of the Chinese workers who were brought to California to build the railroad also sought work in the cities when it was completed. Earlier immigrants greeted them with hostility, however, when jobs became scarce in the 1870s because of a depression. Led by Denis Kearney, Irish immigrants became the core of the **Workingmen's party,** a political organization that blamed the railroad and the Chinese for their economic difficulties.

Small farmers opposed to the railroad allied through the Grange movement. In 1879 the Grangers and the Workingmen's party called California's second constitutional convention in hopes of breaking the power of the railroad. The new constitution they created mandated regulation of railroads, utilities, banks, and other corporations. An elected state Board of Equalization was set up to ensure the fairness of local tax assessments on railroads and their friends, as well as their enemies. The new constitution also prohibited the Chinese from owning land, voting, and working for state or local government.

The railroad soon reclaimed power, however, gaining control of the agencies created to regulate it and, spurred on by the discovery of oil in the Los Angeles area, pushing growth in Southern California. Nonetheless, the efforts made during this period to regulate big business and control racial tensions became recurring themes in California life and politics.

THE PROGRESSIVES

The growth fostered by the railroad eventually produced a new middle class. The economy grew more urban and more diverse, encompassing merchants, doctors, lawyers, teachers, and skilled workers, who were not dependent on the railroad. Nor were these groups tolerant of the corrupt practices and favoritism of the machine, which many thought was holding back the economic development of their communities. Instead, the new middle class demanded honesty and competence, which they called "good government." In 1907 a number of these crusaders established the Lincoln-Roosevelt League, a reform group within the Republican party, and became part of the national **Progressive** movement. They elected their leader, Hiram Johnson, to the governorship in 1910, and they also captured control of the state legislature.

To break the power of the machine, the Progressives introduced reforms that have shaped California politics to this day. Predictably, they created a new regulatory agency for the railroads and utilities, the Public Utilities Commission (PUC); most of their reforms, however, were aimed at weakening the political parties as tools of bosses and machines. Instead of party bosses handpicking candidates at party conventions, the voters were given the power to select their party's nominees for office in **primary elections. Cross-filing** further diluted party power by allowing candidates to file for and win the nominations of more than one political party. The Progressives made city and county elections **non-partisan** by removing party labels from the ballot altogether. They also created a **civil service** system to select state employees on the basis of their qualifications rather than their political connections.

Finally, the Progressives introduced **direct democracy,** which allowed the voters to amend the constitution and make law through initiatives and referenda and to recall, or remove, elected officials before their terms expired. Supporters of an initiative, referendum, or recall must circulate petitions and collect a specified number of signatures of registered voters before it becomes a ballot measure or proposition.

Like those of the Workingmen's party before them, most Progressives were concerned about immigration. Antagonism toward recently arrived Japanese immigrants (72,000 by 1910) led the Progressives to ban land ownership by aliens and to support the National Immigration Act of 1924, which effectively halted Japanese immigration. More positive changes under the Progressives included the right to vote for women, child labor and workers' compensation laws, and conservation programs to protect natural resources.

The railroad political machine eventually died, although California's increasingly diverse economy probably had as much to do with its demise as the Progressive reforms did. The emergent oil, automobile, and trucking industries gave the state important alternative means of transportation and shipping. The reform movement waned in the 1920s, but the Progressive legacy of weak political parties and direct democracy opened up California's politics to its citizens, as well as to individual candidates with strong personalities and powerful interest groups.

THE GREAT DEPRESSION AND WORLD WAR II

California's population grew by more than 2 million in the 1920s (Table 1.1). Most of the newcomers headed for Los Angeles, where employment opportunities in shipping, filmmaking, and manufacturing (clothing, automobiles, and aircraft) abounded. Growth continued at a slower pace during the Great Depression of the 1930s, bringing thousands of poor white immigrants from the nation's Dust Bowl. Many wandered through California's great Central Valley in search of work. They soon displaced Mexicans, who earlier had supplanted the Chinese and Japanese, as the state's farm workers. Racial antagonism ran high, and many Mexicans were arbitrarily sent back to Mexico. Labor unrest reached a crescendo in the early 1930s, as workers on farms, in canneries, and on the docks of San Francisco and Los Angeles fought for higher wages and an eight-hour workday.

TABLE 1.1

CALIFORNIA'S POPULATION GROWTH, SELECTED DECADES, 1850–2000

YEAR	POPULATION	PERCENTAGE OF U.S. POPULATION
1850	93,000	0.4
1900	1,485,000	2.0
1950	10,643,000	7.0
1960	15,863,000	8.8
1970	20,039,000	9.8
1980	23,780,000	10.5
1990	29,733,000	11.7
2000	33,871,648	12.6

SOURCE: U.S. Census.

The immigrants and union activists of the 1920s and 1930s also changed California politics. Many registered as Democrats, thus challenging the dominant Republicans. The Depression and President Franklin Roosevelt's popular New Deal helped the Democrats become California's majority party in registration, although winning elections proved more difficult. Their biggest boost came from Upton Sinclair, a novelist, a socialist, and the Democratic candidate for governor in 1934. His End Poverty in California (EPIC) movement almost led to an election victory, but the state's conservative establishment spent an unprecedented $10 million attacking and ultimately defeating him. The Democrats finally gained the governorship in 1938, but their candidate, Culbert Olson, was the only Democratic winner between 1894 and 1958.

World War II revived the economic boom; California's radio, electronics, and aircraft industries grew at phenomenal rates. The jobs brought new immigrants, including many African Americans. Although their proportion of the state's population doubled during the 1940s, African Americans were on the periphery of racial conflict. Meanwhile, suspected of loyalty to their ancestral homeland, 111,000 Japanese Americans were sent to prison camps during the war. Mexican Americans, too, were victimized when Anglo sailors and police attacked them in the "Zoot Suit Riots" in Los Angeles in 1943.

While the cities boomed, the Central Valley bloomed, thanks to water projects initiated by the state and federal governments during the 1930s. Dams and canals brought water to the desert and reaffirmed agriculture as a mainstay of California's economy. The defense industries that supplemented California's industrial base during the war became permanent fixtures, with aerospace and electronics adding to their momentum.

Although the voters had chosen a Democratic governor during the Depression, they returned to the Republican fold as the economy revived. Earl Warren, who symbolized a new breed of Republican, was elected governor in 1942, 1946, and 1950, becoming the only individual ever to win the office three times. Warren used cross-filing to win the nominations of both parties and staked out a relationship with the voters that he claimed was above party politics. A classic example of California's personality-oriented politics, Warren left the state in 1953 to become chief justice of the U.S. Supreme Court.

POSTWAR POLITICS

In 1958, with the Republican party in disarray because of infighting, Californians elected a Democratic governor, Edmund G. "Pat" Brown, and a Democratic majority in the state legislature. To prevent Republicans from taking advantage of cross-filing again, the state's new leaders immediately outlawed that electoral device.

In control of both the governor's office and the legislature for the first time in the twentieth century, Democrats moved aggressively to develop the state's infrastructure. Completion of the massive California Water Project, construction of the state highway network, and organization of the higher education system were among the advances made to accommodate a growing population. But all these programs cost money, and after opening their pursestrings during the eight-year tenure of Pat Brown, Californians became more cautious about the state's direction. Race riots in Los Angeles and student unrest in Berkeley and elsewhere also turned the voters against liberal Democrats such as Brown.

In 1966 Republican Ronald Reagan was elected governor. Reagan revived the California Republican party and moved the state in a more conservative direction before going on to serve as president. His successor as governor, Democrat Edmund G. "Jerry" Brown, Jr., was the son of the earlier Governor Brown and a liberal on social issues. Like Reagan, however, the younger Brown led California away from spending on growth-inducing infrastructure, such as highways and schools. In 1978 the voters solidified this change with the watershed tax-cutting initiative, Proposition 13 (see Chapter 8). Brown was followed by Republicans George Deukmejian in 1982 and Pete Wilson in 1990, each serving two terms in office. Wilson was initially seen as a moderate, but he moved to the right on welfare, illegal immigration, crime, and affirmative action to win reelection in 1994 and, in the process, alienated many minority voters from the Republican party. In 1998 California elected Gray Davis, its first Democratic governor in sixteen years. He was reelected in 2002.

California voters opted for Republicans in all but one presidential contest between 1948 and 1988, then supported Democrats Bill Clinton in 1992 and 1996 and Al Gore in 2000. Democrats have had more consistent success in the state legislature and the congressional delegation, where they have been the dominant party since 1960. The voters have also been increasingly involved in policymaking by initiative and referendum (see Chapter 2). Amendments to California's constitution, which require voter approval, appear on almost every state ballot. As a consequence, California's 1879 constitution has been amended nearly 500 times; the U.S. Constitution includes just twenty-seven amendments.

Throughout these changes, the state continued to grow, outpacing most other states so much that the California delegation to the U.S. House of Representatives now numbers fifty-three—more than twenty-one other states combined. Much of this growth was the result of a new wave of immigration facilitated by changes in national immigration laws during the 1960s and 1970s. The racially discriminatory quotas introduced by the Progressives in 1924 were eliminated, and immigration from Asia increased greatly, especially from Southeast Asia after the Vietnam War. A national amnesty for illegal residents also enabled many Mexicans to gain citizenship and bring their families from Mexico. In all, 85 percent of the 6 million newcomers and births in California in the 1980s were Asian, Latino, or black.[1] In the 1990s some Californians began leaving the state, but its population continued to increase as a result of births and immigration from abroad.

California's constantly increasing diversity enlivened the state's culture and provided a steady flow of new workers, but it also increased tensions. Some affluent Californians retreated to gated communities; others fled the state. Racial conflict broke out between gangs and in schools and prisons. As in difficult economic times throughout California's history, a recession and recurring state budget deficits in the early 1990s led many Californians, including then-Governor Wilson, to blame immigrants, especially those who were in California illegally. A series of ballot measures raised divisive, race-related issues such as illegal immigration, bilingualism, and affirmative action. The prosperity of the late 1990s and new state leadership muted these issues, but the recession and budget deficits of 2002 threatened to revive them.

CALIFORNIA TODAY

If California were an independent nation, its economy would rank sixth in the world, with an annual gross national product exceeding $1.3 trillion. Much of the state's strength stems from its economic diversity (Table 1.2). The elements of this diversity constitute powerful political interests in state politics.

TABLE 1.2
CALIFORNIA'S ECONOMY

INDUSTRIAL SECTOR	EMPLOYEES	AMOUNT (IN BILLIONS)
Agriculture, forestry, and fisheries	413,000	$ 24.587
Mining	23,600	9.233
Construction	759,200	55.472
Manufacturing	1,822,400	189.962
Transportation, communications, and utilities	721,700	94.183
Wholesale trade	809,800	87.392
Retail trade	2,551,800	121.300
Finance, insurance, and real estate	847,300	293.110
Services	4,679,200	328.274
Government (includes schools)	2,444,800	141.109
Total, all sectors	14,659,800	1,344.623

SOURCE: California Employment Development Department, June 2002. www.edd.ca.gov; and U.S. Department of Commerce, Bureau of Economic Analysis, Survey of Current Business, October 2002.

Half of California–mostly desert and mountains–is owned by the state and federal governments, but a few big farm corporations control the state's rich farmlands. These enormous corporate farms, known as agribusinesses, make California the nation's leading farm state, producing more than 200 crops and providing 45 percent of the fruits and vegetables and 25 percent of the table food consumed nationally. Fresno County alone produces more farm products than do twenty-four states.

State politics affects this huge economic force in many ways, but most notably in labor relations, environmental regulation, and water supply. Farmers and their employees have battled since the turn of the century over issues ranging from wages to safety. Under the leadership of Cesar Chavez and the United Farm Workers union, laborers organized and, supported by public boycotts of certain farm products, achieved some victories for workers, but the struggle continues today. California's agricultural industry is also caught up in environmental issues, including the use of harmful pesticides, the pollution of water supplies, and the urbanization of farmland as booming growth in the Central Valley absorbs farmland and brings urban problems such as traffic to rural areas. The biggest issue, however, is always water. Most of California's cities and farmlands must import water from other parts of the state. Thanks to government subsidies, farmers claim 79 percent of the state's water supply at prices so low that they have little reason to improve inefficient irrigation systems. Meanwhile, urban dwellers are asked to ration water during droughts, and the growth of urban areas is limited by their water supplies. Whether the issue is water, the environment, or labor relations, agriculture is in the thick of California politics as the state strives to protect an essential and powerful industry as well as the interests of its citizens.

Agriculture is big business, but many more Californians work in manufacturing, especially in the aerospace, defense, and high-tech industries. Even more people are employed in postindustrial occupations such as retail sales, finance, tourism, and services. Government policies on growth, the environment, and taxation affect them, too, and all suffer when any one goes into a slump.

The defense industry did just that in the early 1990s, when the federal government reduced spending on expensive military programs and bases following the collapse of communism in the Soviet Union and the end of the Cold War. Suddenly the state had to absorb 17 percent of the defense reductions. Retrenchment cost 175,000 defense-related jobs between 1988 and 1995, amounting to 55 percent of the entire industry sector.[2] Adjusted for inflation, military spending in California today is half what it was in 1988. This negative "peace dividend" coincided with a national recession that encouraged other manufacturers to flee California for states with lower taxes and wages. Altogether, more than 800,000 jobs were lost during the recession of the 1990s.[3]

Although some industries declined, others thrived, especially telecommunications, entertainment, medical equipment, international trade, and above all, high tech. Spawned by the defense and aerospace companies that fell into decline in the early 1990s, high tech was seen as the key to the economic revival of California and the nation at the end of the decade. These highly creative, research-oriented industries focus on computers, electronics, and information management and delivery systems. Today California hosts one-fourth of the nation's high-tech firms, which provide nearly a million jobs.

Half of the nation's computer engineers work in what has been dubbed **Silicon Valley,** after the silicon chip that revolutionized the computer industry. Running between San Jose and San Francisco, Silicon Valley hosts thousands of high-tech firms that invent, manufacture, and market technical instruments, computer chips, networking equipment, workstations, and software. Silicon Valley is also home to thousands of Internet-based "dot-com" businesses. These firms have been joined by biomedical and pharmaceutical companies, all contributing to California's high-tech transformation. So productive is the area that in 1996 it surpassed New York as the top exporting region in the United States.

Silicon Valley's high-tech and Internet industries led California and the nation to an unprecedented economic boom at the end of the 1990s, but high housing costs, inadequate supplies of water, traffic congestion, and environmental regulations led some Silicon Valley companies to transfer production facilities to other states or out of the country altogether. An unquenchable demand for workers, combined with the problems of housing, traffic, and government regulation, pushed the high-tech industry into politics. Companies formed advocacy groups, and individual entrepreneurs spoke out about issues ranging from housing and transportation to producing an educated workforce and increasing the immigration quotas for high-tech workers from abroad. Meanwhile, nearly 20,000 high-tech companies emerged in Southern California, from Santa Barbara ("Silicon Beach") to the San Fernando Valley ("Tech Corridor") to biotechnology-oriented San Diego. The greater Sacramento area in the Central Valley also became home to high-tech manufacturing.

Computer technology also spurred rapid expansion of the entertainment industry, which has long been a key component of California's economy. This particularly benefited the Los Angeles area, which was hit hard by cuts in defense spending, but San Francisco also developed as a multimedia center. Entertainment and tourism together provide more than 500,000 jobs for Californians. Half of these are in the film industry, but tourism remains a bastion of the economy, with California regularly ranking first among the states in visitors. Along with agriculture, high-tech, telecommunications, and other industries, these businesses made California a leader in both international and domestic trade. California's exports totaled $107 billion in 2001—more than 10 percent of the state's total business activity; 47 percent of this trade was technology related.[4]

But the bubble burst in 2001 as the state and nation slumped into recession. Factors beyond California started the slide and the terrible events of September 11, 2001, in New York City, Washington, D.C., and Pennsylvania exacerbated it, but California made its own unique contributions to what became a worldwide recession. First, the California-centered Internet boom went bust as thousands of dot-com companies failed to generate projected profits. The entire high-tech industry went into decline, and thousands of workers lost their jobs. At about the same time, an energy crisis hit California. The state had deregulated energy suppliers in 1996 at the urging of industry, but by 2000, prices for gas and electricity had risen and shortages of electrical power hit parts of the state. The crisis climaxed in the summer of 2001, when Governor Gray Davis directed the state to purchase electricity supplies in advance and to accelerate the construction of more than forty new power plants. These actions resolved the crisis for the moment, but Governor Davis's initial caution and the exorbitant prices the state paid for its advance purchases caused his popularity to slump just as the 2002 election approached. Recalling the rhetoric and policies of the Workingmen's party and the Progressives, some political leaders called for greater regulation or even public ownership of power supplies.

California seemed mired in recession in 2002, as unemployment reached 6.4 percent statewide and 7.6 percent in Silicon Valley (the U.S. rate was 5.9 percent). Precipitously declining tax revenues produced a state budget deficit exceeding $20 billion. California has regularly suffered recessions before and recovered, thanks to the diversity of its economy and its people and their ability to adapt to change. Most other states lack these advantages; some are dependent on a single industry or product.

California's adaptability may derive from a population even more varied than its economy. The succession of immigrant groups has brought workers eager to take jobs in the state's new and old industries. Currently, 26 percent of California's population is foreign born. The extent of California's ethnic diversity, both now and in the future, is indicated in Table 1.3. As of the year 2000, non-Latino whites no longer constituted the majority. Also of note is the shifting ethnic balance among children younger than 14 years of age. Asian and Latino numbers have grown rapidly since the 1970s while the black and white proportions of California's population have fallen. This shift is slowly producing a shift in political power as well.

The realization of the California dream is not shared equally among these groups. In 2001 the income of 12.6 percent of Californians fell below the federal poverty level (compared with 11.7 percent nationwide). The gap between rich and poor in California is among the largest in the United States and is still growing. Poverty is worst among Latinos, blacks, and Southeast Asians, who tend to occupy the bottom of the class structure with low-paying service jobs; other Asians, along with Anglos, predominate in the more comfortable professional classes. The

TABLE 1.3
CALIFORNIA'S RACIAL AND ETHNIC DIVERSITY: PAST, PRESENT, AND PROJECTED

	1990		2000		2010	
	TOTAL	AGE 0–14	TOTAL	AGE 0–14	TOTAL	AGE 0–14
Non-Latino white	57.1%	46.1%	46.7%	36.6%	44.8%	29.7%
Latino	26.0	32.9	32.4	43.6	34.9	49.2
Asian/Pacific Islander	9.2	10.8	11.2	12.4	13.3	14.6
Black	7.1	9.1	6.4	6.9	6.4	6.1
Native American	0.6	1.1	0.5	0.5	0.6	0.4

SOURCE: California Department of Finance, U.S. Census and RAND (www.ca.rand.org), California Population by Race/Ethnicity and Age. Percentage totals may exceed 100 due to rounding; 2000 totals do not include 2.7 percent of mixed race.

economic disparities are profound. Whereas median household income in 1999 was $53,734 for whites and $57,144 for Asians, the median for Latinos was $36,532 and $34,956 for blacks. The 2000 Census also reported that the gap between rich and poor had grown in the 1990s.

The biggest economic problem for minorities, recent arrivals, and many other Californians today is the cost of housing. With a median price of $323,700 in 2002, California houses cost more than double the national average; only 28 percent of the state's families earned enough to purchase the median-priced house.[5] As a result, home ownership in California lags well behind the national average, and more Californians are driven into the rental market–where prices also exceed the national average. Health care is also a problem for poor and working Californians. Twenty-four percent have no health insurance, although coverage has recently expanded under the state's Healthy Families program.

Geographic divisions complicate California's economic and ethnic diversity. The most pronounced of these lies between north and south. The San Francisco Bay Area tends to be liberal and Democratic, with high concentrations of European and Asian ethnic groups. "The City" of San Francisco is a major financial center, whereas its more populous neighbor, San Jose, hosts the high-tech industries of Silicon Valley. Southern California originally drew mainly midwestern immigrants, but today ethnic minorities outnumber Anglos in both the city and the county of Los Angeles. Although Los Angeles tends to vote Democratic, most of the rest of Southern California is staunchly Republican.

Rapid growth in other parts of California now challenges the predominance of the two great metropolitan areas. The state's vast Central Valley has led the way, with cities from Sacramento to Fresno and Bakersfield gobbling up farmland. The Inland Empire, from Riverside to San Bernardino, has grown even more rapidly in the last decade. Although still sparsely populated, California's northern coast, Sierra Nevada, and southern desert regions are also growing, while retaining their own distinct identities. Water, agriculture, and the environment are major issues in all these areas. Except for Sacramento, the Central Valley and these other regions of California are more conservative than their metropolitan counterparts. Their impact on state politics increased greatly in the 1990s.

INTO THE FUTURE

All these factors add up to California politics today. No wonder it seems complicated! From a history full of conflicting interests and turbulent change, California has forged unique political institutions, including weak parties and an electorate that makes policy via direct democracy. All the elements of today's economic, demographic, and geographic diversity vie with one another for political influence within the framework they have inherited, sometimes trying to change it. Just as the economic and demographic changes of the past have shaped contemporary California, so today's changes are shaping the future.

Notes

1. U.S. Census.
2. "The 'Silver' Age of State's Defense-Aerospace Economy," *Los Angeles Times,* July 7, 1996, pp. M1, M6.
3. *New York Times,* March 29, 1995.
4. California Trade and Commerce Agency.
5. California Association of Realtors.

Learn More on the World Wide Web

Demographic data:
California Department of Finance: www.dof.ca.gov
RAND: www.ca.rand.org
U.S. Census: www.census.gov

Learn More at the Library

Mark Baldassare, *A California State of Mind,* Berkeley: University of California Press, or www.ppic.org, 2002. Developments in public opinion.

Carey McWilliams, *California: The Great Exception,* Berkeley: University of California Press, 1949 (or any of his other books).

Frank Norris, *The Octopus,* New York: Penguin, 1901. A novel of nineteenth-century California.

Kevin Starr, *California Dream Series,* Oxford: Oxford University Press. A series of books covering California history from 1850 to 1950 so far.

Working Partnerships USA and Economic Policy Institute, *Walking the Lifelong Tightrope: Negotiating Work in the New Economy,* San Jose: Working Partnerships USA, 1999. www.atwork.org

CHAPTER 2

POLITICAL PARTIES AND DIRECT DEMOCRACY: TOO MUCH DEMOCRACY?

In most states, political parties link citizens and government, building coalitions of different interests and assisting in communicating the positions of candidates to voters. This is not the case in California, where party organizations are weak, the party label means little to voters, and the electorate itself can make policy. As noted in Chapter 1, the Progressive reformers attempted to rid California of the railroad-dominated political machines and bosses of the nineteenth century by weakening political parties. In the resulting power vacuum, personal appeal, skillful media manipulation, and well-financed campaigns have become more important than the political party labels attached to individual candidates.

The Progressives also introduced direct democracy. Through the initiative, referendum, and recall, the voters were given the power to make law and even to overrule leaders or to remove them between elections. Contrary to the reformers' intent, however, interest groups and politicians have learned to dominate the process.

Weak political parties and direct democracy are fixtures of the state constitution and remain very much a part of modern California politics. Some political observers argue that the result promotes political disarray, governmental gridlock, and voters who are confused or turned off. Others believe that the system reflects a political value system that eschews organization and structured authority.

THE PROGRESSIVE LEGACY

To challenge the dominance of the Southern Pacific Railroad's political machine, Progressive reformers from both the Democratic and Republican parties focused on the machine's control of party conventions, where candidates were nominated for office. Republican reformers scored the first breakthrough in 1908 by getting many antirailroad candidates nominated and elected to the state legislature. In 1909 the reform legislators replaced party conventions with **primary elections,** through which the registered voters of each party choose the nominee. Candidates who win their party's primary in these elections face the nominees of other parties in the November **general election.** By instituting this system, the reformers ended the railroad company's monopoly in the nomination process.

In 1910 the Progressives elected a reform governor and legislature. They introduced **direct democracy**–the initiative, referendum, and recall–to give policymaking authority to the people. They replaced the party column ballot–which had permitted block voting for all the candidates of a single party by making just one mark–with separate balloting for each office. They also introduced **cross-filing,** a voting method that permitted candidates of one party to seek the nominations of rival parties. Finally, the Progressives made the election of judges, school board members, and local government officials nonpartisan by eliminating party labels for these contests.

These changes reduced the railroad's control of the political parties, but they also sapped the strength of the party organizations. By allowing the voters to circumvent an unresponsive legislature, direct democracy paved the way for interest groups to dominate policymaking. Deletion of the party column ballot encouraged voters to cast their ballots for members of different parties for different offices (split-ticket voting), increasing the likelihood of divided-party government (see Chapter 7). Nonpartisan local elections made it difficult for the parties to build their organizations at the grassroots level.

Parties tried to regain control of nominations by settling on favored candidates before the primary elections. This effort developed largely through unofficial party organizations, such as the California Republican Assembly (formed in 1935) and the California Democratic Council (formed in 1953), whose influences peaked during the 1960s, when the legislature outlawed such **preprimary endorsements.** Meanwhile, in 1959, the legislature, controlled by Democratic majorities for the first time in more than forty years, outlawed cross-filing, which had been disproportionately helpful to Republican incumbents.

California traditionally held primary elections in June, close to the times of the primaries of the other states. However, during the 1980s many states moved their primaries to early in the year, giving them more say over presidential nominations. To counter that influence, California moved its presidential primary to March in the 1996 election, but gained little because eight other states shifted their primaries to even earlier dates. The state legislature is currently considering moving the primary closer to the November general election in non–presidential election years.

PARTY ORGANIZATION–STRUCTURE AND SUPPORTERS

As a result of the Progressive changes, political parties in California operate under unusual constraints. Although the original reformers have long since departed from the scene, the reform mentality remains very much a part of California's political culture.

THE OFFICIAL PARTY STRUCTURE

According to the California State Elections Code, political parties can place candidates on the ballot by registering a number of members equal to 1 percent of the state vote in the most recent gubernatorial election or by submitting a petition with signatures amounting to 10 percent of that vote. After a party is qualified, if it retains the registration of at least 1 percent of the voters or if at least one of its candidates for any statewide office receives 2 percent of the votes cast, that party will be on the ballot in the next election. By virtue of their sizes, the Democratic and Republican parties have been fixtures on the ballot almost since statehood.

Minor parties, sometimes called **third parties,** are another story. Some have been on the ballot for decades; others have had brief political lives. In 1996, for example, the Reform and Natural Law parties attained ballot status by petition. Although qualifying for the ballot is relatively easy for new parties, breaking the hold of the two major political parties has proved difficult. In the 2002 general election, the Green, American Independent, Natural Law, and Libertarian parties each secured the minimum 2 percent vote for one of their statewide candidates, guaranteeing them positions on the ballot in 2004. The Reform party failed to capture the minimum but qualified by registration numbers for the 2004 presidential race. The Peace and Freedom party, which began as an anti–Vietnam War party in 1968, quietly slipped away after failing to win 2 percent of the vote in the 1998 election.

Despite the existence of several parties on the ballot, the two major parties dominate the state's political landscape. The Democratic and Republican presidential candidates garnered 95 percent of the vote in 2000, although discontent with the Democratic and Republican candidates for governor in 2002 caused the two main parties' share of the vote to drop to 90 percent.

California voters choose their party when they register to vote, which must be done thirty days or more before the election. In 2002, 80 percent were signed up as either Democrats or Republicans. Five percent signed up with the other parties, and 15 percent declared themselves independent (officially known as "decline to state"). The independent percentage has been rising since 1986, when it stood at 9 percent.

California has a **closed primary** system. Voters who are registered with a political party can cast their ballots in the primary only for that party's nominees for various offices. People who specify no party preference when they register can choose which party's primary they wish to vote in. All are free to cast ballots for any party's candidates in the November general election. This system changed briefly in 1996, when a voter-approved initiative introduced the **blanket primary,** which allowed voters to support any listed candidate for each office irrespective of the voters' party affiliations. Proponents praised this new method as an opportunity for voters to nominate the best-qualified individuals; opponents countered that the system would allow voters of one party to pick the candidates of the other–possibly "setting up" a weak nominee for defeat by another party's candidate. But in June 2000 the U.S. Supreme Court declared that the blanket primary violated the First Amendment rights of the state's political parties. With that decision, California returned to its closed primary system.

Before the Great Depression, California was steadfastly Republican, but during the 1930s voters here, like those in many other states, forged a Democratic majority. Since then the Democrats have dominated in registration (Figure 2.1), although their lead has declined from a peak of 60 percent in 1942 to 45 percent in 2000. Republicans have gained from this slippage, but the "decline to state" category has grown most. Registration patterns and voting practices often differ markedly, however. For example, despite their registration margin, the Democrats did not gain a majority in both houses of the state legislature until 1958. More dramatically, Republican candidates have won six of the past ten gubernatorial elections.

As with registration and voting, state law dictates party organization. Today's Democratic and Republican parties have similar structures, although the Democrats elect a few more party officials. The state **central committee,** with about 1,000 members, is the highest-ranking body in each party. All party candidates and officeholders are automatically members, along with county chairpersons. The Democrats also elect members from each assembly district. Each party's state central committee elects a state chair, but it must rotate the position between Northern and Southern California every two years. Although the position traditionally has been powerless, competition for it is often intense.

Beneath the state central committees are county central committees. The voters registered with each party choose committee members every two years in the primary election. Officeholders are also members, which, critics say, enables incumbents to dominate the grassroots members, but the overlapping membership of officeholders, nominees, and county chairs is the only link between the county and state levels of the party. The Progressive reforms rendered California's political parties next to impotent, denying meaningful roles to official organizations and their central committees in preprimary endorsements or fundraising. Nevertheless, county central committees sometimes engage in intense

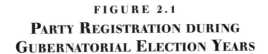

FIGURE 2.1

PARTY REGISTRATION DURING GUBERNATORIAL ELECTION YEARS

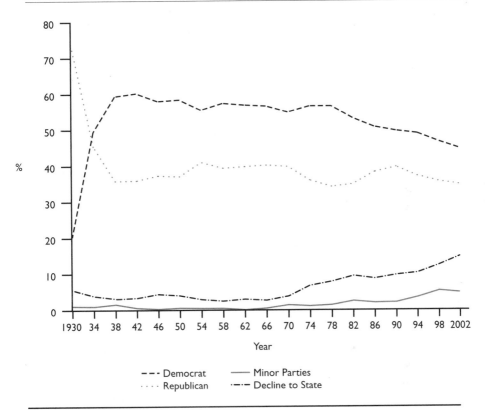

SOURCE: California Secretary of State.

conflict among activists. Liberals usually dominate Democratic county central committees, whereas conservatives enjoy disproportionate power in Republican committees. The religious right gained influence in the Republican party in the 1990s by organizing to take over a majority of the party's county central committees. Recently, moderate Republicans have successfully challenged their control in some counties.

California's political parties got a chance to strengthen their role in choosing party nominees (a major source of their weakness) when the U.S. Supreme Court overturned the state ban on preprimary endorsements of candidates by political parties in 1990. California Democrats responded quickly by establishing a preprimary endorsement process that required a candidate to secure at least 60 percent of the delegates at their state convention, but the Republican party has officially declined to utilize preprimary endorsements.

Despite assertions of better party organization, preprimary endorsements have mattered little to California voters. Of sixteen statewide candidates officially endorsed by the Democrats in primaries since the court ruling, nine were incumbents certain of victory and four of the others failed to win their party's nomination. Whether the preprimary endorsement will strengthen the parties is doubtful because California's weak parties are a consequence not only of state law but also of fickle voter loyalty to the parties, split-ticket voting, high-spending campaigns, and the media.

PARTY SUPPORTERS

Activists in the official and unofficial party organizations make up less than 5 percent of the electorate. The remaining support base comes from citizens who designate their party affiliations when they register to vote and usually cast their ballots accordingly. Both major parties enjoy widespread support, but the more liberal Democratic party fares better with blacks, city dwellers, union members, and residents of Los Angeles, Sacramento, and the San Francisco Bay Area. Central California was once dominated by the Democrats, but increasingly the region has become a battleground for the two major parties. Latino voters have also traditionally favored Democrats, a tendency that has been strengthened by Republican support for several statewide initiatives on welfare, immigration, affirmative action, and bilingual education. Most Asian nationalities identify themselves as Democratic, but some (notably Chinese and Vietnamese) lean Republican. Chinese, Vietnamese, and Asian Indians are also more likely to register as independents than are other Californians. As with Latinos, Asian loyalties to the California Republican party were weakened by its sponsorship of initiatives perceived as anti-immigrant in the 1990s. Thanks in large part to the failure of Republicans to win support from minority voters, Democrats currently enjoy majorities in the state legislature and congressional delegation and control of all statewide offices except one.

The more conservative Republican party does better with whites, suburbanites, residents of rural areas, and Southern Californians (except in Los Angeles), as well as with older, more affluent voters and with Christian conservatives. Together these constituencies are the most dependable voters, which is one reason why Republicans have won elections in California despite their registration disadvantage. Republican strategist Stuart Spencer, however, warns, "The general electorate has gone exactly the other way from the party leadership in terms of positions on immigration, ethnicity, abortion, guns. Till they get their ship righted, and move back to a more centrist, moderate position, they're going to have trouble."[1]

DIRECT DEMOCRACY

Party politics is not the only way by which Californians participate in the political process. To counter the railroad machine's control of state and local government, the Progressive reformers also guaranteed the people some say through the mechanisms of direct democracy introduced in Chapter 1: the recall, the referendum, and the initiative.

Each statewide initiative or referendum is assigned a number by the secretary of state; local issues are assigned letters by the county clerk. Propositions once started with the number 1 in each election, but beginning in 1983, to prevent confusion, they continued in sequence up to Proposition 227 in June 1998. In November of that year, numbering started over again with Proposition 1.

THE RECALL

The least-used Progressive reform is the **recall,** a means by which the voters can remove officeholders at all levels of government between scheduled elections. Recall advocates simply circulate a petition with a statement of their reasons, which can be anything at all. They must collect a specific number of voter signatures within a specific time period, the numbers of which vary with the office in question. A recall petition for a state executive officeholder, for example, would require a number of signatures equal to 12 percent of the vote in the last election within 160 days, whereas 20 percent is necessary for judicial or legislative recalls. At the local level, recall requirements vary between 10 and 30 percent over periods of between 40 and 160 days.

If enough signatures are collected by advocates and validated by the secretary of state (for a state officeholder) or by the county clerk (for a local officeholder), an election is held. The ballot is simple: "Shall [name] be removed from the office of [title]?" The recall takes effect if a majority of voters vote yes, and either an election or an appointment, whichever state or local law requires, fills the vacancy for the office. Elected officials who are recalled cannot be candidates in the replacement election.

The recall has been used most extensively and successfully in local government, particularly by angry parents against school boards. Even so, only a dozen or so recalls are on local ballots in any single year and only about half of the officials who face recall are removed from office. Although state officeholders are occasionally threatened with recall, no one was removed from 1914 to 1995, when two recall efforts succeeded when Democrats and Republicans were fighting over control of the state assembly. Since then, there have been no other successful recalls of elected state officials. Although rarely used, the recall remains a powerful weapon for discontented constituents—or scheming politicians.

THE REFERENDUM

The **referendum** is another form of direct democracy. One version of referendum allows voters to nullify acts of the legislature. Advocates of a protest referendum have ninety days to collect a number of signatures equal to 5 percent of the votes cast for governor in the previous election (419,260, based on the 1998 vote). Protest referenda are rare. A recent example occurred in 2000, when the insurance industry used referenda and persuaded voters to reject regulations imposed on it by the legislature.

THE INITIATIVE

Recalls and referenda are reactions to what elected officials do; in contrast, the **initiative** allows voters to make policy themselves. They can do so by drafting a new law or a constitutional amendment and then circulating petitions to get it onto the ballot. Qualifying a proposed law requires a number of signatures equal to 5 percent of the votes cast for governor in the last election; constitutional amendments require a number of signatures equal to 8 percent (670,816, based on the 1998 election). If enough valid signatures are obtained within 150 days, the initiative goes to the voters at the next election or, on rare occasions, in a special election called by the governor.

Initiatives tend to be the most controversial measures on the ballot. Their subjects vary wildly. In the past few years, Californians have voted on property tax limits, minimum wage hikes, capital punishment, affirmative action, gun control, AIDS quarantines, insurance reforms, illegal immigration, and Indian casinos, to name a few. Sometimes initiative proposals can be sweeping in design. For example, in 1993 and 2000 voters turned down a school voucher program that would have set aside public funds to be spent on each child in the school (public or private) designated by his or her parents. Among the several initiatives in 1998, voters passed limits on bilingual education and banned the slaughter of horses for human consumption. In 2000 the electorate voted to define marriage as a relationship between a man and a woman only.

Twenty-four other states provide for the initiative, but few rely upon it as readily as California. The use of initiatives flourished between 1912 and 1939. Then, after four decades of relative dormancy, political consultants and special interest groups rediscovered the initiative and ballot measures proliferated. The 1988 and 1990 election year ballots witnessed an explosion, with eighteen initiatives each. In 2002 the March and November elections combined produced only five initiatives (Table 2.1).

LEGISLATIVE "INITIATIVES," CONSTITUTIONAL AMENDMENTS, AND BONDS

Propositions may also be placed on the ballot by the state legislature. These usually equal or exceed the number of citizen-generative

TABLE 2.1
THE TRACK RECORD OF STATE INITIATIVES

TIME PERIOD	NUMBER	NUMBER ADOPTED	NUMBER REJECTED
1912–1919	31	8	23
1920–1929	34	10	24
1930–1939	37	10	27
1940–1949	20	7	13
1950–1959	11	1	10
1960–1969	10	3	7
1970–1979	24	7	17
1980–1989	52	25	27
1990–1999	50	20	30
2000–2002	20	7	13
Totals	289	98 (34%)	191 (66%)

SOURCE: California Secretary of State.

initiatives. Such **legislative initiatives** may include new laws that the legislature prefers to put before the voters rather than enact on its own or proposed constitutional amendments for which voter approval is compulsory. Voter approval is also required when the governor or the legislature wishes to borrow money to finance parks, schools, transportation, or other capital-intensive projects through the sale of bonds (state IOUs). Few of these proposals are controversial, and more than 60 percent are passed. In 2002, for example, voters approved five bonds totaling $21.5 billion for new schools, parks, water projects, and housing.

Most legislative initiatives are on the ballot because the legislature cannot amend the constitution or borrow money without public approval. Sometimes, however, the legislature turns to the voters because lawmakers don't want to make controversial policy without public support. This was the case in 1993, when voters were asked to make permanent a then-temporary half-cent addition to the state sales tax.

THE POLITICS OF BALLOT PROPOSITIONS

The recent proliferation of ballot propositions is hardly the result of sudden democratic participation. It stems largely from the opportunism of special interests, individual politicians, and public relations firms. California's state lottery, for example, was virtually the creation of a single company that paid for the circulation of petitions and then funded the campaign that sold the proposition to the voters. Similarly, the 1994 initiative attempt to weaken the state's antismoking provisions was circulated and sponsored almost entirely by a single tobacco company. It was easily defeated at the polls. Perhaps the most ironic interest group/ballot proposition relationship occurred in 2000, when leading insurance company associations maneuvered two protest referenda onto the ballot only to spend $50 million to ensure their defeats! Why? This roundabout route preempted legislative intervention.

State ballot propositions can be costly endeavors. Although intended as mechanisms for grassroots citizen groups to shape policy, even the most grassroots of initiatives costs half a million dollars to qualify, and millions more are required to mount a successful campaign. Campaigns for and against the fourteen propositions on the ballot in 1998 cost $227.1 million, up 61 percent from the $141.3 million spent in 1996. Much of the increase occurred because of the $96 million spent on Proposition 5, a proposal allowing the development of casinos on Indian land, by Indian tribes and Nevada gambling interests—the most ever spent on a single proposition in California history. Sometimes initiatives are funded primarily by wealthy individuals, such as international financier George Soros (drug decriminalization) and high-tech executive Tim Draper (school vouchers). In 2002 movie star Arnold Schwarzenegger sponsored an initiative to fund after-school programs. Politicians have also discovered initiatives as a way to further their own careers or shape public policy. For example, Republican Governor Pete Wilson helped secure reelection in 1994 by sponsoring a successful measure on illegal immigration. Democratic Governor Gray Davis has also embraced the initiative as a public policymaking vehicle, leading the fight for passage of a 2000 initiative that lowered the required margin for local school bonds from two-thirds to 55 percent.

Public relations firms and political consultants—virtual "guns for hire"—have developed lucrative careers from managing initiative and referenda campaigns. One consultant, for example, made more than $2 million working for the "Yes on 5" Indian casino initiative in 1998, simply for obtaining enough signatures to qualify the proposal for the ballot.[2] Other specialists offer expertise in public-opinion polling, computer-targeted mailing, and television advertising—the staples of modern campaigns. Some firms generate initiatives themselves by conducting test mailings and preliminary polls in hopes of snagging big contracts from proposition sponsors. With millions of dollars in campaign spending in the balance, big economic interests gain an advantage over grassroots efforts—surely not what the Progressives intended.

Nevertheless, direct democracy offers hope to the relatively powerless by enabling them to take their case to the public over the opposition of elected officials. In 1998 entertainer Rob Reiner led a successful effort to add fifty cents to the price of each pack of cigarettes, with the additional money directed to children's health programs. Tobacco allies spent more than $30 million against Proposition 10, compared with less than $10 million spent by the advocates. That such groups can beat long odds and the state's political establishment only increases the attractiveness of initiatives.

Unfortunately, direct democracy does not necessarily result in good law. Because self-interested sponsors draft initiatives and media masters run campaigns, careful and rational deliberation is rare. Flaws or contradictions in successful initiatives may take years to resolve. Sometimes this is done through the implementation of the measures by government agencies or through the legislative process. Increasingly, however, disputes about initiatives are tested in state and federal courts, which must rule on whether they are consistent with other laws and with the state and federal constitutions. In recent years courts have overturned all or parts of initiatives dealing with illegal immigration and campaign finance, for example. Although such rulings seem to deny the will of the voters, the courts are doing their jobs. Even the voters cannot make laws that contradict the state or federal constitutions.

The increased use of direct democracy has also had an impact on the power of our elected representatives. Although we expect them to make policy, their ability to do so has been constrained by a sequence of initiatives in recent decades. This is particularly the case with term limits, budgeting, and taxing, as we will see in Chapter 8.

The proliferation of initiatives, expensive and deceptive campaigns, flawed laws, and court interventions have annoyed voters and policymakers alike. Perhaps as a consequence, two-thirds of all initiatives are rejected (Table 2.1). Nevertheless, 56 percent of the respondents to a recent statewide survey "believe that policy decisions made through the initiative process are probably better than policy decisions made by the governor and legislature."[3] Even larger majorities favor reform of the initiative process, including more public information about the funding of initiative campaigns and review of ballot language and legal issues before initiatives are placed on the ballot.[4]

POLITICAL PARTIES, DIRECT DEMOCRACY, AND CALIFORNIA POLITICS

Direct democracy and weak political parties are basic to California politics. The direct primary maximizes voter choice among candidates; weak parties foster high-spending, candidate-centered campaigns that often seem to confuse or obscure voter choice. Candidates must rely on financial contributors to pay for campaigns that are not funded by the parties, thus enhancing the influence of individuals and groups with money. Direct democracy gives these same interests yet another way to advance their causes, and the proliferation of propositions further confounds voters. Does California have too much democracy? Sometimes it seems so. Some voters feel overwhelmed and turned off, but most manage to sift through complex initiatives and seductive campaigns to find the policies and candidates who suit their preferences.

Notes

1. *New York Times*, February 28, 2000.
2. *Sacramento Bee*, January 24, 1999, p. 1A.
3. "Just the Facts: Californians and the Initiative Process," Public Policy Institute of California (www.ppic.org), February 2001.
4. Mark Baldassare, "Californians and Their Government," Public Policy Institute of California (www.ppic.org), January 2001.

Learn More on the World Wide Web

About political parties:

American Independent Party: www.aipca.org

Democratic party: www.ca-dem.org

Green party: www.cagreens.org

Libertarian party: www.ca.lp.org

Natural Law party: www.natural-law.org

Reform party: www.reformparty.org

Republican party: www.cagop.org

About ballot propositions:

www.calvoter.org

www.ss.ca.gov

Learn More at the Library

Ann O'M Bowman and Richard C. Kearney, *State and Local Government: The Essentials*, New York: Houghton Mifflin Company, 2000.

Elisabeth R. Gerber, et al., *Stealing the Initiative*, Upper Saddle River, NJ: Prentice Hall, 2001.

Richard J. Ellis, *Democratic Delusions: The Initiative Process in America*, Lawrence: University Press of Kansas, 2002.

Jim Shultz, *The Initiative Cookbook*, San Francisco: The Democracy Center, 1996.

Political Action Handbook, California Journal, 1999.

VOTERS, CANDIDATES, CAMPAIGNS, AND THE MEDIA: THE MIX OF MONEY AND MARKETING

■════════■

A typical California ballot requires voters to make decisions about more than twenty elective positions and propositions. Even the best-informed citizens sometimes find it difficult to choose among candidates for offices they know little about and to decide on obscure and complicated propositions. Because political parties provide little guidance, candidates, campaigns, and the media play crucial roles in this process in California.

Campaigns and the media are also important because of the mobility and rootlessness that characterize California society. More than half of all Californians were born elsewhere, and as many as one-third of the voters in every state election are participating for the first time. Residents also move frequently within the state, reducing the political influence of families, friends, and peer groups and boosting that of campaigns and the media.

THE VOTERS

California residents who are eighteen years or older are eligible to vote unless they are in prison or a mental institution. New voters must register at least fifteen days before an election by completing a simple form available at public places such as post offices, fire stations, and shopping centers, where party activists eagerly solicit new voters. Registering became even easier in 1995, when federal "Motor Voter" legislation required states to offer voter registration along with applications for driver's licenses and at social service agencies.

Altogether, more than 21 million Californians are eligible to vote, but only 15 million register and about 11 million actually vote. That's just over half of all those eligible–close to the national average. In the gubernatorial election of 2002, however, turnout among those registered to vote hit a record low 46 percent. Turnout is usually higher in presidential elections, and in 2000, 68 percent of the state's registered voters participated, a rate that was nevertheless lower than the national average. Although most voters cast their ballots at their designated polling places, California leads the nation in voting by mail, with 25 percent of the electorate requesting absentee ballots from their county registrars of voters in recent years. Some do so because they expect to be away from home or will be too busy on election day, others because they want to deal with the complex ballots at their leisure, and still others because they are pushed to vote by mail by campaigns trying to make sure their supporters vote.

Why do so many Californians neglect to vote? Some people don't get around to registering. Some are too busy on election day. Some are apathetic, some are unaware, and others feel too uninformed to act. Still others believe that voting is a charade because "it's all rigged" or "the candidates are all alike." Some people are bewildered by all the messages that bombard them during a typical California election. But the reason that people most frequently give for not voting is that they are too busy.

Yet political campaigns are designed to motivate voters to support candidates and causes. This task is complicated because those who vote are not a representative cross section of the actual population. Non-Latino whites, for example, make up 46.7 percent of the population but 71 percent of the electorate. Although Latinos, African Americans, and Asians constitute 53.3 percent of California's population, they are 29 percent of the voters in primary and general elections.[1] This low turnout is not due merely to apathy, however. Among Latinos, for example, one-third are too young to vote, and another third are not citizens. Latino turnout has more than trebled since 1990, however, rising from 4 percent of the electorate to 14 percent in 2000.[2] The surge was fueled by Republican attacks on immigrants and affirmative action, tactics that resulted in Democrats winning a greater share of the Latino vote than ever before.

Differences in the levels of participation do not end with ethnicity. The people most likely to vote are suburbanites and Republicans who are richer, better educated, and older. Lower levels of participation are usually found among poorer, less educated, and younger inner-city residents and Democrats. People over the age of fifty-five, for example, constitute 26 percent of the state's population but 35 percent of the voters.[3] With a voting electorate that is more conservative than the population as a whole, Republicans can win statewide elections despite the Democratic edge in registration and liberal ballot measures rarely pass.

THE CANDIDATES

When we vote, we choose among candidates, but how do candidates come forward in the first place? Some are encouraged to run by political parties or interest groups seeking to advance their causes. Political leaders looking for allies recruit others. Such recruited candidates are less common in California than elsewhere because of the state's weak political parties and wide-open political structures. Most California candidates are just individuals with an interest in politics who make up their own minds to run and then seek support. The rising cost and increasing negativity of campaigns have discouraged some people from running, although wealthy individuals who can fund their own campaigns have appeared more frequently as candidates in recent years. Most candidates start at the bottom of the political ladder, running for school board or city council, and work their way up, building support as they go. Wealthy candidates usually try to leapfrog this apprenticeship, but the voters tend to be skeptical about their lack of political experience, especially when they are seeking high office. Businessman Al Checchi, for example, spent $38 million of his own money running for governor in 1998 but couldn't win his party's nomination.

Historically, California candidates have been even less representative of the population than is the electorate. The vast majority have been educated white males of above-average financial means. Only in the 1970s and 1980s did increasing numbers of women, minorities, and gays and lesbians begin to win nominations and elections. All of these groups remain underrepresented in relation to their presence in the electorate.

The 1990s brought change, however. Underrepresented groups grew in strength and organization, and structural changes facilitated their candidacies. A 1990 initiative limited the number of terms that legislators could serve, thus ensuring greater turnover in the state legislature; in addition, the reapportionment of legislative districts after the censuses of 1990 and 2000 resulted in redrawn legislative districts that gave Latino candidates new opportunities and added a total of eight more seats to California's congressional delegation.

Latinos gained the most from these changes, including a sizable delegation in the legislature and the election of Cruz Bustamante as lieutenant governor in 1998 and 2002. Latinos have also gained representation at the local level, with more than 20 percent of California's county supervisors, city council members, and mayors being Latino (double their numbers of a decade ago).

Although a smaller minority, African Americans got a foothold in state politics earlier, including the statewide positions of lieutenant governor and superintendent of public instruction. As the longest-serving speaker of the state assembly (1980–1995), Willie Brown was for many years one of California's most powerful politicians. He is now mayor of San Francisco. Another African American, Herb Wesson of Los Angeles, is currently speaker of the assembly, but overall, black representation has shrunken as other minorities have gained in numbers. Less than 5 percent of California's county supervisors, city council members, and mayors were African American in 2001.

Asian Americans, however, are the most underrepresented of California's racial minorities, holding just over 3 percent of county supervisor, city council member, and mayoral positions and few state legislator positions. Some Asian Americans have, however, won election to statewide offices in the past, including Secretary of State March Fong Eu (1974), U.S. Senator S. I. Hayakawa (1976), and California State Treasurer Matt Fong (1994). But electing candidates has been particularly difficult for Asian Americans because many are recent immigrants for whom political involvement is just beginning and because cultural and political differences exist among the many groups in the Asian community, notably the Chinese, the Japanese, the Vietnamese, the Filipinos, and the Koreans.

Women candidates have been more successful. Both of California's U.S. senators are now women, and women have been elected to statewide office in the past, although none are currently serving. A substantial number of women are in the state legislature, however, and 37 percent of California's city council members, mayors, and county supervisors are women.

Lesbians and gays achieved electoral office later than any of these groups. Greater bias may be a factor, and the closeted status of many homosexuals—including candidates and elected officials—also weakens organizing efforts and may render gay and lesbian successes invisible. More than thirty openly gay and lesbian individuals now hold state or local offices, including a growing number of state legislators.

Sexism and racism partly explain the underrepresentation of all these groups, but other factors also contribute. Many members of these groups are economically disadvantaged, which makes it hard to participate in politics, let alone to take on the demands of a candidacy. Minorities also have difficulty winning support outside their own groups and may alienate their "natural constituencies" in the process. California's weak political parties provide little assistance. The fact that minorities are less likely to vote than Anglos further reduces their candidates' potential.

CAMPAIGNING CALIFORNIA STYLE

The introduction of primary elections in 1909 shifted the focus of campaigns from political parties to individual candidates; other reforms weakened the parties further and accelerated the "individualization" of campaigns. As a result, political aspirants raise money, recruit workers, research issues, and plot strategy on their own or with the help of expensive consultants rather than with that of political parties, which contribute little in the way of money or staff. California campaigns thus tend to focus on the personalities of the candidates rather than on parties or policies.

Weak parties mean that candidates must promote themselves, so the cost of running for state assembly or senate often exceeds $1 million, and campaigns for statewide offices are even more expensive. The candidates for governor spent a total of $100 million in 1998 and even more in 2002 (see Table 3.1 for totals).

The money for campaigns is provided by interest groups, businesses, and wealthy individuals (see Table 4.3 for the top group contributors to the 1998 gubernatorial campaigns). Much campaign financing is provided by **political action committees (PACs),** through which interest groups direct substantial sums of money to preferred campaigns. Legislative leaders such as the speaker of the assembly and the president pro tem of the senate raise huge sums from such sources and channel the money to their allies in the legislature, whereas individual candidates raise money by asking potential contributors directly and through special fundraising events, ranging from coffees and barbecues to banquets and concerts. They also solicit contributions from specific audiences through targeted mailings and the Internet. Some wealthy candidates provide their own funds—Bill Simon "loaned" $10 million to his unsuccessful 2002 campaign for governor—but most must rely on donors with an interest in the outcome of the election.

Worried about the influence of all this money and turned off by campaign advertising, Californians have approved a series of initiatives aimed at regulating campaign finance. The **Political Reform Act of**

TABLE 3.1

CALIFORNIA CAMPAIGN SPENDING FOR LEGISLATIVE AND STATEWIDE OFFICES, GUBERNATORIAL ELECTION YEARS, 1978–1998 (IN MILLIONS OF DOLLARS)

YEAR	LEGISLATURE	STATEWIDE OFFICES
1978	21.26	23.77
1982	44.00	36.07
1986	64.20	49.30
1990	54.61	87.53
1994	78.42	107.11
1998	86.66	174.72

SOURCE: Secretary of State (www.ss.ca.gov).

1974 required public disclosure of all donors and expenditures. Since then, reformers have tried repeatedly to limit the amount individuals and groups can contribute, but initiatives approved by the voters have been invalidated by the courts on grounds that they unduly limited free speech. In 2000 the voters approved Proposition 34, a legislative initiative setting higher limits than previous measures ($3,000 for legislative candidates, $5,000 for statewide, and $20,000 for governor). These limits applied for legislative candidates beginning in 2001 but for statewide candidates only after the 2002 election. Proposition 34 also set voluntary spending limits for candidates.[4] California campaigns have nevertheless become the most costly in the nation. Other states have avoided California's fate by finding other ways to limit the influence of money in politics, including twenty-four states that provide public financing for campaigns.

Meanwhile, to get around reforms, political parties, interest groups, and PACs have begun paying independently for ads and mailings for their favored candidates and causes. Such **independent expenditures**—about which candidates are not supposed to be informed—have increased greatly in recent years and often feature the most vicious attacks on opponents.

WHAT THE MONEY BUYS

Campaign contributors expect their money to buy immediate access and long-term influence. Candidates deny making specific deals, however, insisting that they and their contributors merely share views on key issues. Millions of dollars flow into candidates' coffers through this murky relationship. Energy and utility companies, for example, gave generously to candidates, including Governor Gray Davis, when the state was shaping and reshaping its energy policies. Revelations about such contributions and others from donors with business before the state caused problems for Davis's 2002 reelection campaign, although he won nevertheless.

So much money is needed because California campaigns, whether local or statewide, are highly professionalized. This is nothing new in California politics. In fact, California publicists Clem Whitaker and Leone Baxter virtually invented modern, mass-media campaigns back in 1934 when they coordinated the media attack on Upton Sinclair, the left-leaning Democratic candidate for governor. To compensate for weak party organizations, candidates hire consultants and management firms to perform virtually all campaign activities, including recruiting workers, raising money, advertising, and conducting public opinion polls. These specialists understand the workings of California's volatile electorate and use their knowledge to a candidate's benefit.

Television has made campaign management firms indispensable, allowing candidates instant entry into as many homes as there are in the viewing area. It also enables candidates to put their messages across at exactly the moment of their choosing–between wrestling bouts, during the news or *Oprah,* or just after *Friends,* depending on the specific targeted audience. The efficacy of the medium is proved repeatedly when little-known candidates spend big money on television commercials and become major contenders, as did Al Checchi in the 1998 gubernatorial campaign and Bill Simon in 2002.

Recent studies report that "nine of every ten California voters judge candidates and issues mainly by the advertising they see on television, whereas in more compact, less populous states, the proportion drops to two of every three."[5] No wonder television advertising now accounts for roughly 80 percent of all spending for statewide races. In a state as big as California, however, it is the only way to reach the mass of voters. Little-known candidates like Checchi or Simon can make themselves known statewide in weeks. At the height of the 1998 gubernatorial primary, candidates were running an average of 527 ads a day in California's major media markets.[6] Approximately $127 million was spent on 119,492 television ads in 2000.[7] Well-funded initiative campaigns also rely heavily on television advertising. The two sides of the 1998 proposition on Indian gambling, for example, spent a total of $47 million on television alone.

Television is too costly for most candidates for legislative and local office, however. A thirty-second prime-time spot costs $10,000 to $20,000 in Los Angeles, and because most TV stations broadcast to potential audiences much larger than the individual districts (875,000 people in a state senate district and 437,000 in an assembly district), the message is wasted on many viewers. Advertising during the day or on small stations or cable can be much cheaper, however, and many legislative candidates have turned to these media. Most, however, have found a more efficient way to spend their money: **direct mail.** Computers have revolutionized political mail by enabling campaign strategists to target selected voters with personal messages.

Direct-mail experts develop lists of voters and their characteristics and then send special mailings to people who share particular qualities. In addition to finding out each voter's party registration and residence, these experts use carefully compiled data banks to identify various groups, including liberals and conservatives; students, ethnic voters, and retired people; homeowners and renters; union members; feminists and gays; and even those most likely to vote. After the targets have been identified, campaign strategists can pitch just the right message to them. Conservatives may be told of the candidate's proposals to "get tough on crime"; liberals may be promised action on environmental protection. For the price of a single thirty-second television spot, local or legislative candidates can do a districtwide mailing, reaching only their selected audiences.

Lately, candidates have taken their campaigns to the Internet, setting up Web sites to provide information and using email to communicate with the media and with supporters. Only two campaigns posted Web sites during the 1994 election, but more than 300 did so in 2000.[8] Some campaigns have used Web sites to recruit volunteers and raise money. Having a Web site is virtually expected of candidates now, but the political impact of this new medium is probably minimal. Whereas TV and mail enable the candidates to reach us whether we're interested or not, voters must initiate contact on the Internet themselves, which limits the audience to those who are already interested. The California Teachers Association, however, used email to campaign against a proposition on school vouchers in 2000, asking its thousands of members to forward the message to their own lists, and 2002 Republican gubernatorial candidate Bill Simon targeted emails to Christian conservatives seeking their support and then urging them to vote.

Television and direct mail dominate California campaigns because they are the best means of reaching masses of voters, but the use of these media is not without problems. Because they are expensive, campaign costs have risen, as has the influence of major donors. Candidates who are unable to raise vast sums of money are usually left at the starting gate. Incumbent officeholders, who are masters at fundraising and are familiar with the issues important to contributors, become invincible. Furthermore, these media are criticized for leading to the oversimplification of issues and an emphasis on the negative. Television commercials for ballot measures often reduce complicated issues to emotional thirty-second spots aimed at uninformed voters. Candidates' ads and mailings indulge in the same oversimplification, often in the form of attacks on opponents. Negative ads, or "hit pieces," are frequently launched at the last minute, leaving the victims unable to respond. When the candidates portray each other negatively, as in the 2002 race for governor between Gray Davis and Bill Simon, voters often feel that they must choose the lesser evil rather than make a decision on the policies and positive traits of either candidate. In the primary election that year, Davis spent $9 million on television ads discrediting Dick Riordan, a potential Republican opponent he thought would be tougher to beat than Simon, thus helping Simon win the Republican nomination. The voters seem to have grown skeptical of such attacks, yet they are sometimes hard to resist. Campaign consultants, who are usually blamed for the phenomenon, point out that campaigns had a nasty edge even a century ago and that the public pays more attention to negative messages than to positive ones.

Overall, California's media-oriented campaigns reinforce both the emphasis on candidates' personalities and voter cynicism. Some people blame such campaigns for declining voter turnout. Contemporary campaigns may also depress voter turnout by aiming all their efforts at regular voters and ignoring those who are less likely to vote—often minority voters. Although this is a sensible way to use campaign resources, it is not a way to stimulate democracy.

Some candidates try to revive old-fashioned door-to-door or telephone campaigns and get-out-the-vote drives on election day. Labor union volunteers, for example, helped State Assemblyman Gil Cedillo win a tough special election in Los Angeles in 1998. Grassroots campaigns have a long and honorable tradition in California, but even in small-scale, local races, they are often up against not only big-money opponents but also the California lifestyle: Few people are at home to be contacted, and those who are may be mistrustful of strangers at their doors. For good or ill, candidates need money for their campaigns; those with the most money don't always win, but those with too little rarely even become contenders.

THE MEDIA IN CALIFORNIA POLITICS

In addition to their role in campaigns, the mass media transmit almost everything that Californians know about politics. They have a profound impact on ideas, issues, and leaders. Until the 1950s a few family-owned newspapers dominated the media. Then television gave the newspapers some competition while expanding the cumulative clout of the mass media.

PAPER POLITICS

California's great newspapers were founded in the nineteenth century by ambitious men such as Harrison Gray Otis of the *Los Angeles Times,* William Randolph Hearst of the *San Francisco Examiner,* the de Young brothers of the *San Francisco Chronicle,* and James McClatchy of the *Sacramento Bee.* Their families controlled these newspapers for a century and remain influential today.

These print-media moguls used their newspapers to boost their communities, their political candidates, and their favored causes. Most were like Otis, an ardent conservative who fought labor unions and pushed for growth while making a fortune in land investments. In the heyday of bossism, his *Los Angeles Times* supported the Southern Pacific's political machine and condemned Progressive leader Hiram Johnson as a demagogue, as did many other newspapers in the state. Other journalists, however, founded the Lincoln-Roosevelt League and led the campaign for reform.

Even after reform triumphed over the machine, newspapers continued to play a crucial role in California politics. In Los Angeles, San Francisco, Oakland, San Jose, and San Diego, Republican publishers used the power of the press–on both the editorial and the news pages–to promote their favorite candidates and causes. They were instrumental in keeping Republicans in office long after the Democrats gained a majority of registered voters.

Change came only in the 1970s, when most of the California's family-owned newspapers became part of corporate chains. The new corporate managers replaced the newspapers' old employees, whom they often viewed as hacks, with professional editors and reporters drawn from a national pool of career journalists. News coverage became more objective, and opinion was more consistently confined to the editorial pages. Even the editorials changed, sometimes endorsing Democrats and liberal positions. Meanwhile, the number of daily newspapers published in California declined. Once there were hundreds, and every city had several competing with one another. Today, ninety-five survive, and most cities have just one. Some competition remains, however, as major metropolitan dailies invade one another's turf and as suburban weeklies proliferate. The latter, however, almost never cover state politics.

TELEVISION POLITICS

Newspapers also changed because of competition from television. A 2000 public opinion survey reported that 44 percent of Californians said they got their news and information about state politics from TV, with 35 percent citing newspapers, 10 percent radio, and 4 percent the Internet.[9] But when it comes to covering California politics, television leaves a lot to be desired.

Except for the Sacramento stations, not one of California's TV stations operates a news bureau in the state capital. Television news editors shy away from state political coverage because they believe that viewers want glamorous national stories or local features. In contrast, twenty newspapers employ capital correspondents, many of whom are political specialists. Broadcast journalists, by comparison, are usually "generalists," lacking the expertise to understand or explain a story or to probe into it.

The minimal TV coverage of state politics–a tiny percentage of newscast time, according to various studies–is mainly drawn from newspaper articles, wire service stories, or events staged by politicians. Most elected officials employ press secretaries to help them get coverage, and on some occasions they fly around the state to get free exposure. Four stops suffice because broadcast stations in Los Angeles, San Francisco, San Diego, and Sacramento reach 85 percent of the state's viewing public.

In recent gubernatorial campaigns, even such visits often did not get candidates on the local news. Most TV stations around the state declined to broadcast candidate debates live out of fear of low ratings. Coverage is so poor that one newspaper declared that it constituted "another California innovation: the all-commercial political campaign."[10] Cynics pointed out that if TV doesn't provide news coverage, candidates are forced to buy advertising time—on TV. The top two Los Angeles television stations, for example, averaged just 35 seconds a night in news coverage during the month before California's 2000 presidential primary election—but they received $5.6 million for ads for candidates.[11]

REPORTING ON CALIFORNIA

Newspapers may be heading in the same direction. Sports, movie stars, and plane crashes make the front page; stories on state politics are usually buried in the newspapers' second sections. TV newscasts, however, may ignore state politics entirely.

Although television has abandoned Sacramento except to drop in now and then to cover big stories live by satellite, every major newspaper in the state maintains a Sacramento bureau; the *Los Angeles Times* fields the largest and most respected contingent. Critics say that the press corps still tends to run in a pack, reporting the same stories rather than probing for others, but whatever its shortcomings, coverage of California politics is better today than it once was. Whereas reporters were once the politician's pals and the publisher's tools, today's journalists are mostly skilled professionals who seek to tell their stories accurately and objectively. Their relations with elected officials are more distant and strained than in the past.

One notable change is the increase in investigative reporting—the publication of long stories, sometimes in series, that may significantly affect public policy or individual politicians. Election coverage has also improved. The old promotion of favorites has been replaced by more balanced reporting that incorporates public opinion polls, computer analyses of campaign finances and voting patterns, and critiques of TV commercials.

Newspapers still promote their political favorites, although the format has changed. Once the personal prerogative of publisher-owners, endorsements today are usually given by editorial boards rather than by individuals. They are also generally confined to the editorial pages rather than splashed throughout the entire newspaper. Republican candidates and conservative causes are still more likely to win a paper's editorial blessings, but the pattern is less consistent than it once was. The influence of these endorsements has declined, however, because people now have other sources of information, most notably television and direct mail.

The traditional print and broadcast media still dominate, but more alternatives are becoming available to Californians. Latino newspapers and television and radio stations reach major audiences, especially in Southern California. Many sites on the Internet focus on politics, and citizens anywhere in the state can read newspapers elsewhere online or access state or local governments (see "Learn More on the World Wide Web" at the end of each chapter). Citizens can even watch their government in action on the California Channel, now available on 114 cable systems.

ELECTIONS, CAMPAIGNS, AND THE MEDIA

A mercurial electorate and weak political parties make the influence of money and media greater in California politics than in other states. Politicians must organize their own campaigns, raise vast sums of money, and then take their cases to the people via direct mail and television. Such campaigns are inevitably personality-oriented, with substantive issues taking a back seat to puff pieces or attacks on opponents. The media provide a check of sorts, but television news emphasizes personalities rather than issues or ideas, and newspapers, although offering more complete coverage, no longer capture the public's attention as they once did.

All of this takes us back to the issue of declining voter turnout. Could stronger parties and issue-oriented campaigns revive voter participation? Maybe, but both campaign consultants and the media say they are already giving the public what it wants.

Notes

1. California Opinion Index, January 2002, The Field Institute.
2. Voter News Service.
3. Public Policy Institute of California, "Just the Facts," March 2001, www.ppic.org.
4. $400,000 in the primary and $700,000 for candidates for assembly; $600,000 in the primary and $700,000 for candidates for senate; $6 million in the primary and $10 million for candidates for governor.
5. *New York Times,* October 14, 1994.
6. *Washington Post,* May 29, 1998.
7. *San Jose Mercury News,* December 29, 2001.
8. California Voter Foundation (www.calvoter.com).
9. Public Policy Institute of California, January 2000 (www.ppic.org).
10. *New York Times,* May 6, 1998.
11. "Dollars vs. Discourse in 2000 Presidential Primaries," Alliance for Better Campaigns (www.bettercampaigns.org).

Learn More on the World Wide Web

Public opinion polls:

Los Angeles Times: www.latimes.com/news/custom/timespoll/

Public Policy Institute of California: www.ppic.org

Elections:

California Journal: www.statenet.com/news/calj/

California Secretary of State: www.ss.ca.gov

California Voter Foundation: www.calvoter.com

Campaign Finance: www.campaignfinancesite.org

League of Women Voters: www.ca.lwv.org

Smart Voter: www.smartvoter.org

Learn More at the Library

Campaigning in California, California Journal (on campaign finance regulations).

Gerald C. Lubenow, ed., *California Votes: The 1998 Governor's Race,* Berkeley: IGS Press, 1999.

Greg Mitchell, *The Campaign of the Century,* New York: Random House, 1992. Upton Sinclair's 1934 campaign for governor.

Chapter 4

INTEREST GROUPS: THE POWER BEHIND THE DOME

Most people belong to one or more **interest groups,** organizations formed to protect and advance shared objectives of their members. Existing in all shapes and sizes, interest groups range from labor unions, ethnic organizations, and business associations to student unions and automobile clubs.

Amid California's diversity, interest groups have prospered, proliferated, and become more important than political parties to many Californians. More people pay dues to the California Teachers Association (CTA) or the California Chamber of Commerce, for example, than contribute to the state Republican or Democratic parties. California's political institutions provide a fertile political environment for group power. Weak political parties make candidates dependent on groups for financing while direct democracy enables groups to make policy. Interest groups also successfully influence legislators in the lobbies beneath the capitol dome. Some observers view these efforts as assisting the legislative process; others see them as manipulating that process. All groups are not equal, however; depending on resources and issues, some are far more successful than others.

THE EVOLUTION OF GROUP POWER IN CALIFORNIA

The astonishing length of California's constitution attests to the historical clout of the state's interest groups. In other states, groups gain advantages such as tax exemptions through state law, which can be changed by the legislature at any time. In California, such protections are often written into the constitution, making them more difficult to alter because constitutional amendments require the approval of the electorate. Among

California's constitutionally favored interests are dozens of crops (protecting organized agriculture), trees less than forty years old (protecting the timber industry), and ships for passengers or freight (protecting the shipping industry). These "safeguards" were not responses to public outcry; interest groups pushed them through for their own benefit.

Until well into the twentieth century, California politics catered to one powerful group after another. First it was the mining industry, followed by ranching and agriculture. From about 1870 until 1910 the Southern Pacific Railroad monopolized the state's economy. After the railroad, a diverse group of industries held sway until about 1960. Land development, shipping, and horse racing were prominent early in this period, followed by the automobile and defense industries. Agricultural interests have remained strong through all these periods.

By the 1960s both the players and the game had changed. Economic diversification continued, with service and leisure industries supplementing manufacturing and the emergence of high-tech industries from defense and aerospace. Insurance companies, physicians' and attorneys' groups, and other vocation-related associations actively lobbied state government for favored status. Single-issue groups, such as Gun Owners of California and Mothers Against Drunk Driving (MADD), joined the fray, as did minority, feminist, and gay and lesbian organizations. Along with these came a new wave of reformers, led by "public interest" groups such as Common Cause.

Group politics in California today is wide open, with every imaginable interest making its claim, facilitated by the state's political system. As a consequence, California politicians often find themselves responding to the demands of interest groups rather than governing them.

THE GROUPS

Interest groups vary in size, resources, and goals. At one extreme, groups that pursue economic benefits tend to have relatively small memberships but a great deal of money, whereas public interest groups often have large memberships but little money. A few, such as the Consumer Attorneys of California (CAC; trial lawyers), have the double advantage of being both large and well funded.

ECONOMIC GROUPS

Economic groups predominate. Every major corporation in the state, from the Southern Pacific to Standard Oil and from the Bank of America to Apple Computer, is represented in Sacramento either by their own lobbyists or by lobbying firms hired to present their cases to policymakers.

Often, individual corporations or businesses with similar goals form associations to further their general objectives. Such umbrella organizations include the California Manufacturers and Technology Association, the California Business Alliance (for small enterprises), the California Bankers Association, and the California Council for Environmental and Economic Balance (utilities and oil companies). The California Chamber of Commerce alone boasts 12,000 members.

Agribusiness is particularly active because farming depends on government on issues such as water and pesticides. The giant farming operations maintain their own lobbyists, but various producer groups also form associations. Most of the state's wine makers, for example, are represented by the 550-member Wine Institute. Broader organizations such as the California Farm Bureau, one of the state's most powerful lobby groups, speak for agribusiness in general.

Recently, high-tech industries have asserted their interests in issues ranging from Internet taxation to transportation and education. Organizations such as TechNet, the Silicon Valley Manufacturing Group, and the American Electronics Association have lobbied for regulatory changes, tax relief, relaxed smog emissions rules, and other changes. During the first half of 2002 alone, California-based Siebel Systems contributed $2.1 million to various state and national campaigns, with Intel, Sun Microsystems, Hewlett-Packard, VeriSign, and eBay also becoming political active.

PROFESSIONAL ASSOCIATIONS AND UNIONS

With public policy affecting so much of what they do, professional associations such as the California Medical Association (CMA), the California Association of Realtors (CAR), and the CAC are among the state's most active groups, and they regularly hover among the largest campaign contributors. Other professionals, such as chiropractors, dentists, and general contractors, also maintain active associations. Because all these professionals serve the public, many tend to promote their concerns as broader than self-interest. Their credibility is further enhanced by expertise in their respective fields and by memberships of large numbers of affluent, respected individuals.

Teachers' associations and some other public employee organizations fall somewhere between business associations and labor unions. Their members view themselves as professionals but in recent years have increasingly resorted to traditional labor union tactics, such as collective bargaining and strikes. The CTA is the major education group in Sacramento. Other public workers, such as the highway patrol and state university professors, have their own organizations, but the California State Employees Association (CSEA) is the giant among these groups, with more than 137,000 active members and the ability to raise large campaign war chests when necessary. It regularly ranks with the CMA, CAR, and CAC among the top campaign contributors in the state.

Traditional labor unions representing nurses, carpenters, auto workers, and dozens of other occupations are also active, although with only 17 percent of California's workers as members, unions are less powerful here than in some other states. Still, they have their moments, as in 1996, when the California Federation of Labor, an umbrella organization for most of the state's unions, successfully led an initiative campaign to raise the state's minimum wage. Perhaps the most successful union of all is the California Correctional Peace Officers Association, which contributed more than $600,000 to the reelection campaign of Governor Gray Davis in 2002 and saw the governor sign a three-year pay increase of 33 percent in the midst of a huge state budget deficit.[1]

DEMOGRAPHIC GROUPS

Another set of groups that depends more on membership than on money can be described as **demographic groups.** Based on characteristics that distinguish their members from other segments of the population, such as their ethnicity, gender, or age, such groups usually have an interest in overcoming discrimination. Most racial and ethnic organizations fall into this category.

Virtually all of California's minorities have organizations to speak for them. One of the earliest of these was the Colored Convention, which fought for the rights of blacks in California in the nineteenth century. Today several such groups advocate for African Americans, Asians, and Native Americans. The United Farm Workers (UFW), the GI Forum, the Mexican American Legal Defense Fund (MALDEF), and the Mexican American Political Association (MAPA) represent Latinos.

The National Organization for Women (NOW) and the National Women's Political Caucus (NWPC) actively support women candidates and feminist causes. Both groups have organized better at the local level than at the state level, however. The same may be said of gays and lesbians, except when disputing what were viewed as antigay initiatives in 1978, 1986, 1988, and 2000.

Age groups play a smaller part in state politics, but with an aging population heavily dependent on public services, organizations such as the American Association of Retired Persons (AARP), with no less than 3 million members, have achieved a higher profile in state politics, particularly on health care issues.

All of these groups, whether based on race, age, gender, or sexual orientation, derive their strength almost exclusively from the size of their memberships. Racial, ethnic, feminist, and gay and lesbian organizations, however, have also proved capable of raising big money for selected candidates and causes.

SINGLE-ISSUE GROUPS

The groups discussed so far tend to have broad bases and to deal with a wide range of issues. Another type of interest group operates with a broad base of support for the resolution of narrow issues. **Single-issue groups** push for a specific question to be decided on specific terms. They support only candidates who agree with their particular position on an issue. The California Abortion Rights Action League (CARAL), for example, endorses only candidates who support abortion (or "choice"), whereas antiabortion (or "pro-life") groups work only for candidates who take the opposite stance. Likewise, the Howard Jarvis' Taxpayers Association evaluates candidates and ballot propositions solely in terms of whether they meet the association's objective of no unnecessary taxes and no wasteful government spending.

The specific focus of these groups can be a source of power on occasion, but the reluctance to compromise limits their effectiveness in the give-and-take of state politics. Nevertheless, a group's ability to deliver a solid bloc of voters can affect the outcome of a close election and thus enhance its clout at least on a temporary basis. In recent elections, groups as varied as the National Rifle Association (NRA), Christian conservatives, antiabortion and pro-choice activists, and taxpayers' associations have claimed such an impact.

PUBLIC INTEREST GROUPS

Although virtually all organized interests claim to speak for the broader public interest, some groups clearly seek no private gain and thus more correctly claim to be **public interest groups.** Consumer groups, for example, campaign for the public interest in the marketplace. Some such groups have pushed for insurance reform, whereas others, such as Toward Utility Rate Normalization, monitor rate requests by the utilities before the state Public Utilities Commission. Environmental organizations such as the Sierra Club and Friends of the Earth have been particularly active in California on issues such as water management, offshore oil drilling, air pollution, transportation, and pesticide use. Land use is another important concern of these groups, both for private development in sensitive areas and for public lands, which comprise half the state. A recent survey found that one in nine Californians claims to belong to an environmental group.[2]

Other public interest groups, such as Common Cause and the League of Women Voters, focus on governmental reform. These two groups have been involved in several efforts to reform campaign finance in California.

A final type of public interest group isn't really a group at all: local governments. Cities, school districts, special districts, and counties all lobby the state government, upon whose funds they heavily depend, through the League of California Cities, the California School Boards

Association, and the California State Association of Counties (CSAC). Dozens of cities and counties employ their own lobbyists in Sacramento, as do other governmental agencies. They also endorse ballot measures affecting their interests and, on rare occasions, even sponsor initiatives, but unlike other groups, cities and counties cannot make campaign contributions or organize their constituents.

TECHNIQUES AND TARGETS: INTEREST GROUPS AT WORK

The goal of interest groups is to influence public policy. To do this, they must persuade policymakers. The legislature, the executive branch, the courts, and sometimes the people are thus the targets of the various techniques these groups may use.

LOBBYING

The term **lobbying** refers to the activity that once went on in the lobbies outside the legislative chambers. Group advocates would buttonhole legislators on their way in or out and make their cases. This still goes on in the lobbies and hallways of the capitol, as well as in nearby bars and restaurants and wherever else policymakers congregate.

Until the 1950s lobbying was a crude and disreputable activity. Lobbyists lavished food, drink, gifts, and money on legislators. Artie Samish, the prototype for modern lobbyists, perfected the craft first by learning about state government as a legislative staffer and then by representing breweries, unions, racetracks, banks, railroads, tobacco corporations, and the chemical industry. Operating with the motto "select and elect," Samish bestowed money on allies and used his knowledge of their personal lives to influence them. "On matters that affect his clients," Governor Earl Warren once said, "Artie unquestionably has more power than the governor."[5] Samish fell from power, however, after his 1953 conviction for income tax evasion.

Today's lobbyists, like Samish, are experts on the legislative process. Many have served as legislators or staff members. They focus on **legislative committees** and leaders, lobbying the full legislature only as a last resort. Unlike their predecessors, lobbyists must be well informed to be persuasive with today's more sophisticated legislators. They still use money, but less crudely than Samish, instead strategically contributing to campaigns. Legislators and lobbyists alike assert that contributions buy access, not votes. But the tie between money and access can be powerful in its own right. In the words of one lobbyist, their influence is "most visible in committees when lobbyists are giving testimony. The

TABLE 4.1

LOBBYING IN CALIFORNIA, 1977–2000 (SELECTED YEARS)

LEGISLATIVE SESSION	NUMBER OF LOBBYISTS	TOTAL AMOUNT SPENT
1977–1978	582	$ 19,640,650
1987–1988	825	158,498,208
1997–1998	2,295	292,615,513
1999–2000	2,176	344,318,650

SOURCE: Secretary of State (www.ss.ca.gov).

committee members sit up and listen when it's someone with clout or money; they pay attention."[4]

All of this makes lobbying not only a highly specialized profession but also an expensive activity, as Table 4.1 indicates. It is also on the increase. Between 1977 and 2000, the number of registered lobbyists in Sacramento almost quadrupled, climbing from 582 to 2,176, including about two dozen former legislators. Most represent one business or group, such as those in Table 4.2. **Contract lobbyists,** who work for several clients simultaneously, are on the rise, however. Kahl/Pownall Advocates, for example, represents insurance companies, General Electric, the California Restaurant Association, the Western States Petroleum Association, and others. With clients paying more than $8.5 million, they were California's top lobbying firm in 1999 through 2000.[5] But whether contract or specialized, more and more lobbyists make a career of their professions, accruing vast knowledge and experience. These long-term professionals became even more powerful when term limits eliminated senior legislators with countervailing knowledge, although some lobbyists complain that term limits means they must constantly reestablish their credibility with new decision makers. One prominent lobbyist, however, explains his lack of concern about term limits or other reforms: "Whatever your rules are, I'm going to win," he says.[6]

Not all lobbying is done by professionals. Some groups can't afford to hire a lobbyist, so they rely on their members instead. Even groups with professional help use their members on occasion to show elected officials the breadth of their support. Usually this sort of lobbying is conducted by individuals who reside in the districts of targeted legislators, although sometimes groups lobby en masse, busing members to the capitol for demonstrations or concurrent lobbying of many elected officials.

Such grassroots efforts by nonprofessionals have special credibility with legislators, but well-financed groups have learned to mimic grassroots groups by forming front groups or "Astroturf" organizations that conceal their real interests. Prison guards, for example, backed "Crime

TABLE 4.2
CALIFORNIA'S TOP TEN LOBBYIST EMPLOYERS, 1999–2000

GROUP	AMOUNT SPENT
California Teachers Association	$5,742,924
Pacific Telesis and subsidiaries	5,160,857
Western States Petroleum Association	3,862,287
California Chamber of Commerce	3,580,571
Edison International and subsidiaries	3,110,820
California Healthcare Association and affiliates	2,699,098
California Medical Association	2,697,448
California Manufacturers Association	2,435,296
State Farm Insurance Companies	2,383,542
Consumer Attorneys of California	2,318,112

SOURCE: Secretary of State (www.ss.ca.gov).

Victims United," and the building industry formed "Californians for Schools."

Although most lobbying is focused on the legislature, knowledgeable professionals also target the executive branch, from the governor down to the bureaucracy. The governor not only proposes the budget but also must respond to thousands of bills that await his or her approval or rejection. The bureaucracy must interpret new laws and future recommendations to the governor. These responsibilities do not escape the attention of astute interest groups.

Lately, the public has become a target of lobbying, too. In media-addicted California, groups have begun making their cases through newspaper and television advertising between elections. Health care, education, abortion, and other issues have been subject to costly media campaigns.

CAMPAIGN SUPPORT

Most groups also try to further their cause by helping sympathetic candidates win election and reelection. Groups with limited financial resources do so by providing volunteers to go door-to-door or to serve as phone bank callers for candidates. Labor unions in Los Angeles and San Jose have been particularly successful at electing candidates they endorse; agricultural organizations in the Central Valley have enjoyed similar successes.

Groups with greater resources make generous campaign contributions. Teachers and other public employee groups, for example, contributed heavily to the campaign of Governor Gray Davis, who subsequently worked toward increasing education spending and public employee pay during his first term. According to a Common Cause study, the top interest group contributor to California candidates in the 1999–2000 electoral cycle was California Correctional Peace Officers Association, followed by the CTA (Table 4.3).

Campaign contributors claim their money merely buys them access to decision makers, but the press and the public often suspect a more conspiratorial process, and evidence of money-for-vote trades has emerged in recent years. FBI agents posing as businessmen asked legislators for favors in exchange for campaign contributions, resulting in the 1994 convictions of fourteen people, including five legislators. Their trials revealed the extent to which legislators hustle lobbyists for contributions. More recently, California's elected insurance commissioner was forced to resign when it was discovered that he let insurance companies accused of wrongdoing avoid big fines by giving smaller amounts to foundations that subsequently spent the money on polls, ads featuring the commissioner, and other activities. As a result of these scandals, politicians and contributors probably exercise greater caution, but the high cost of campaigning in California means that candidates ask and lobbyists give.

LITIGATION

Groups that are not satisfied with the actions of elected officials may take their cases to the courts or the people. **Litigation** is an option when a group questions the legality of legislation, and in recent years many have

---

TABLE 4.3

TOP CAMPAIGN CONTRIBUTORS FOR STATE AND LEGISLATIVE CAMPAIGNS, 1999–2000 (EXCLUDES CONTRIBUTIONS FROM POLITICAL PARTY ORGANIZATIONS)

1. California Correctional Peace Officers Association (CCPOA)	$2,307,565
2. California Teachers Association (CTA)	1,950,538
3. Philip Morris Companies	1,305,194
4. Service Employees International Union	1,235,899
5. California Medical Association (CMA)	1,191,291
6. Edison International	1,066,790
7. Pacific Gas & Electric	1,062,861
8. California Dental Association	1,058,585
9. Agua Caliente Band of Cahuilla Indians	1,050,805
10. California School Employees Association (CSEA)	1,050,135

SOURCE: Common Cause, March 18, 2002 (www.commoncause.org).

turned to the courts for the final interpretation of the law. In court, opponents have challenged successful initiatives such as those on immigration, affirmative action, campaign finance, and bilingual education, hoping that the initiatives would be declared unconstitutional. Even if a group loses its case, it may delay implementation of a new law or at least establish a principle for debate in the future. In 2001 MALDEF challenged the legislature's redistricting plan, claiming underrepresentation of Latinos. Even though MALDEF lost the case, the organization kept the issue in public focus and, as such, a campaign issue in the 2002 election.

DIRECT DEMOCRACY

Hiram Johnson championed the initiative in 1911 "to make every man [sic] his own legislature," but today only broad-based or well-financed groups have the resources to collect the necessary signatures or to pay for expensive campaigns. Direct democracy gives interest groups opportunities to make policy themselves by promoting their proposals through initiatives and referenda.

Every initiative on the ballot represents major organizing efforts and campaign spending by interest groups. In 1998, for example, tribal supporters of gambling on Indian lands spent $10 million qualifying an initiative for the ballot in just thirty days–the most expensive petition campaign in history. The subsequent campaign on the proposition itself also broke records, with the two sides spending a total of $96 million. The voters ultimately approved the initiative.

Recall is also sometimes used by interest groups, although mostly to remove local elected officials. Teachers' unions, conservative Christians, and minority groups have conducted recall campaigns against school trustees, for example. Despite more than 100 attempts to recall state officials, only a handful have qualified for the ballot and only two state legislators have actually been recalled. Both were victims of a 1995 battle between political parties rather than interest groups.

With millions poured into petition drives and election campaigns, direct democracy seems to fall short of the intent of its creators. The voters, however, reject the proposals of moneyed interests with regularity.

REGULATING GROUPS

Free spending by interest groups and allegations of corruption led to Proposition 9, the **Political Reform Act of 1974,** an initiative sponsored by Common Cause. Overwhelmingly approved by the voters, the law requires politicians to report their assets, disclose contributions, and declare how they spend campaign funds. Other provisions compel lobbyists to register with the secretary of state, file quarterly reports on their campaign-related activities, and reveal the beneficiaries of their donations. The measure also established the **Fair Political Practices Commission (FPPC),** an independent regulatory body, to monitor these activities. When the commission finds incomplete or inaccurate reporting, it may fine the violator. Of greater concern than the financial penalty, however, is the bad press for those who incur the commission's reprimand. The voters approved new constraints in 1996, when they enacted strict limits on the interest group practice of rewarding supportive legislators with travel and generous fees for speeches. However, this legislation was soon challenged, creating an atmosphere of uncertainty. In 2000 the voters approved yet another initiative, Proposition 34, which placed new constraints on political action committees while making it easier to infuse "soft money," or indirect contributions, into campaigns.

MEASURING GROUP CLOUT: MONEY, NUMBERS, AND CREDIBILITY

Campaign regulations generally are intended to reduce the disproportionate influence of moneyed interests in state politics. Their changes notwithstanding, economic groups have had the advantage. Their money makes the full panoply of group tactics available to them and also gives them the staying power to outlast the enthusiasm and energy of grassroots groups. Public interest groups and demographic groups, however, gain strength from numbers and credibility from acting on motives other than pure self-interest. Occasionally, they have prevailed, such as in 1998, when children's and health groups overcame a campaign deficit of $27 million to $7 million to pass Proposition 10, a fifty cent per pack cigarette tax dedicated to children's health programs.

Whatever the balance among groups, they are central to California politics. Besides California's weak political parties and its opportunities for direct democracy, California's diversity, with so many groups clamoring for favor, makes that inevitable.

Notes

1. "Davis Gets More Money From Prison Guards," *Los Angeles Times*, March 30, 2002, pp. A1, A13.
2. *PPIC Statewide Survey*, San Francisco: Public Policy Institute of California, June 2000.
3. Quoted in Lester Velie, "The Secret Boss of California," *Collier's*, August 13, 1949, p. 13.

4. Kathy Beasley, "Low-Budget Lobbyists," *California Journal,* September 1988, p. 404.

5. Secretary of State.

6. Douglas Foster, "The Lame Duck State," *Harper's,* February 1994.

Learn More on the World Wide Web

Lobbying or campaign spending:

www.ss.ca.gov

www.calvoter.org

Sample groups:

California Association of Realtors (CAR): www.car.org

California Chamber of Commerce: www.calchamber.com

California Common Cause: www.commoncause.org/states/california

California Labor Federation: www.calaborfed.org

Latino Issues Forum: www.lif.org

League of Women Voters: www.ca.lwv.org

Sierra Club: www.sierraclub.org/chapters/ca

Learn More at the Library

Political Action Handbook, California Journal, Fifth Edition.

Arthur H. Samish and Bob Thomas, New York: *The Secret Boss of California,* Crown, 1971.

Dan Walters and Jay Michael, *The Third House,* Berkeley: Berkeley Public Policy Press, 2002.

CHAPTER 5

THE LEGISLATURE: THE PERILS OF POLICYMAKING

Thousands of bills are introduced in the California legislature every year. Some are trivial, such as establishing rules for tattoo-removal equipment or determining the official ghost town of the state. But along with deciding lightweight issues, the legislature is responsible for solving the state's thorniest problems, such as underfunded public education, inadequate revenues, and a decaying infrastructure. Each year the members write laws and, along with the governor, determine the budget and define services and programs. As the center of such power, the legislature is a natural target of public scrutiny, and criticism of it is understandable. Less understandable, however, is its inability to resolve big issues.

For most of the 1990s the Democratic legislature tangled repeatedly with Republican Governor Pete Wilson on all sorts of issues. The annual budget, perhaps the most pressing of all legislative lawmaking responsibilities, was not enacted on schedule once during the decade. Many legislators suffered further embarrassment in recent years over issues ranging from sexual harassment to income tax avoidance. Not surprisingly, a 1996 public opinion survey found people critical of the state legislature by a three-to-two margin.[1]

The public's attitude toward the legislature began to change toward the end of the decade. By acquiescing to term limits and managing budget surpluses instead of deficits, the legislature began down the slow road to political rehabilitation. By 1999 public approval of the legislature's performance turned decidedly positive, by a two-to-one margin.[2] Nevertheless, by 2002 public opinion was once again evenly divided, no doubt because of the lingering effects of the state's power crisis and the budget shortfall.[3]

THE MAKING AND UNMAKING OF A MODEL LEGISLATURE

California's first constitution provided a **bicameral** (two-house) **legislature** similar to the U.S. Congress. When the constitution was revised in 1879, the senate was fixed at forty members serving four-year terms (with half the body elected every two years), and the assembly was set at eighty members serving two-year terms.

Legislative districts for both houses were originally determined by population, with members representing approximately equal numbers of people. Voters changed the system in 1926 through a constitutional amendment that organized the legislature like the U.S. Congress. Assembly members, like counterparts in the U.S. House of Representatives, were elected on the basis of population, and senators by county in the same way that each state has two U.S. senators.[4] The large number of counties north of the Tehachapi Mountains permitted the North to dominate the state senate despite Southern California's growth. By 1965 twenty-one of the forty state senators in California represented 10 percent of the population; Los Angeles County, home to 35 percent of the state's residents, had but a single state senator.

THE SHIFT TOWARD PROFESSIONALISM

Legislative leadership and organization didn't matter much during the Southern Pacific machine-dominated years (see Chapters 1 and 2). The office of speaker of the assembly, prized today, passed almost casually from one member to another with each new two-year session. Even after the railroad's demise as the dominant political force, the legislature remained vulnerable to numerous powerful interest groups. But the transformation of California pushed the legislature to modernize, too.

The legislature's composition changed radically after the U.S. Supreme Court handed down its ***Reynolds v. Sims*** decision in 1964, which ordered all states to organize the upper houses by population rather than by county or territory. The shift increased urban and southern representation dramatically. After the 1966 elections there were twenty-two new senators and thirty-three first-term assembly members. The new leaders were younger, better educated, and more ideological; more of them were members of racial minorities.

With the court-ordered changes as a backdrop, the voters approved a 1966 ballot proposition to create a full-time legislature with full-time salaries. Until then, the part-time legislature met for no more than 120 days every other year to consider general laws; two-year state budgets were enacted during the in-between years. Since 1967, however, the legislature has met on an average of more than 200 days per year, with salaries to match. As of 2002 the base salary was $99,000 (highest among the fifty states); perks pushed annual incomes near $125,000.[5]

REAPPORTIONMENT: KEEPING AND LOSING CONTROL

Currently, each assembly district has about 437,500 residents; each senate district has about 875,000. Over time, district sizes change with growth and population movements, leading some districts to become much larger than others. So that districts stay relatively equal in size, the legislature realigns districts after the national census, which is conducted every ten years. This seemingly straightforward process, **reapportionment,** has become intensely political in California.

Until 1991, reapportionment occurred after negotiations between the majority and minority parties. With Republican Governor Pete Wilson taking office alongside a legislature with Democratic majorities, however, the process changed. Wilson vetoed the plan that he viewed as overly favorable to the Democratic party. He then appointed a reapportionment commission to draw new district lines, the results of which appeared to aid Republicans. Ultimately, the plan was approved by the state supreme court. Despite Wilson's efforts, the legislature remained in Democratic hands throughout the next decade, except for a slim Republican majority in the assembly during the 1995–1996 session. The state congressional delegation also continued with a Democratic majority, except for a 26–26 tie during the 1995–1996 period.

The 2001 reapportionment took place under different circumstances. With the Democrats controlling both the executive and legislative branches, the redistricting effort was assured a cooperative political environment. As with the pre-1991 effort, Democrats and Republicans agreed on a plan that, while providing equal numbers, basically preserved the status quo. Because of disproportionate population growth in the Central Valley and Southern California, representation increased somewhat in those two areas. However, because the 2001 plan packed strong Democratic or Republican majorities into almost every district, the partisan division of legislature after the 2002 election was almost identical to the pattern before the election.

NEW PLAYERS, NEW RULES

Reapportionment, the change from part-time to full-time, and higher salaries transformed the legislature. The new framework attracted better-educated and more professional individuals and also made elected office more feasible for women and minorities. Thus, in 2003 the assembly included 23 women, 5 African Americans, 15 Latinos, and 5 Asians; the senate included 11 women, 2 African Americans, and 10 Latinos (Figure 5.1).

Despite greater diversity, the legislature has narrowed in terms of vocational backgrounds. During the 1980s, legislative aspirants from the business world were flanked by large numbers of lawyers, local activists, educators, and former legislative aides. But increasingly, the "business candidate" has emerged as the dominant category of self-description. During the 1990s, about half of all legislative candidates on the ballot listed some form of business as their occupations. And beginning in the late 1990s, large numbers from city and county elected posts also took seats in the legislature.[6]

FIGURE 5.1
WOMEN AND MINORITIES IN THE CALIFORNIA LEGISLATURE, 1975–2004

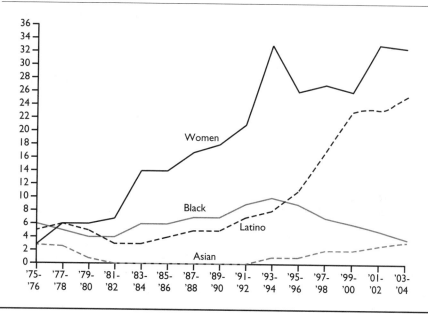

Compiled from The California Almanac of Government and Politics; clerks of assembly and senate.

Much of the legislature's new look stems from rising voter antipathy toward incumbents and the near-certainty of their perpetual reelection. Voter anger peaked in 1990 with the passage of **Proposition 140,** a "term limits" initiative for legislators and statewide elected officials. To guarantee periodic turnover, this measure limited elected executive branch officers and state senators to two four-year terms and assembly members to three two-year terms; it also cut the legislature's operating budget (and thus its staff) by 38 percent. Clearly, California voters thought their legislature had become too professional for its own good.

TERM LIMITS A DECADE LATER

When term limits advocates proposed the concept, they envisioned a "turnstile" type of legislature whose members would be in office for relatively short periods. Such a system was designed to guarantee new faces, reduce the influence of money, and enhance fresh ideas. Of the seventeen states with term limits legislation in place, only Oklahoma's is more restrictive than California.

Early assessments suggest that some reform objectives have been met while others show no sign of coming to pass. New faces have certainly appeared, but in many cases legislators have simply jumped from one house to the other. Although the flow of money into campaign coffers has been slowed, the overall costs of campaigning continue to set new records. As for fresh ideas, the jury is still out. Ironically, a study of the first complete class of assembly members under term limits in 1996 showed remarkable similarity between the new legislators and the so-called professionals who dominated before Proposition 140.[7]

Whereas term limits ensure brief periods of legislative service, there are no limits on the "service" of bureaucrats and lobbyists. Because of their knowledge, nonelected individuals have become increasingly important in shaping the legislative environment. Meanwhile, leadership positions in the legislature, although not as lightly regarded as a century ago, no longer carry the clout that once made the legislature an orderly and effective counterweight to the executive branch.

Nationwide, the term limits movement seems to be abating. Mississippi voters rejected the concept in 1999. In 2002 the Idaho legislature removed term limits and the Oregon State Supreme Court found the state law on term limits unconstitutional. Nevertheless, in March 2002, California voters rejected Proposition 45, a ballot proposition that would have preserved term limits while enabling legislators to add four years. For those seeking a career in public office, term limits remain a death knell.

LEADERS AND FOLLOWERS

Although the two houses share the business of making law, they function differently. The assembly is more hierarchical, with the **speaker** clearly in charge. The speaker controls the flow of legislation, committee chairs and assignments, and vast campaign funds. The number of standing, or topical, committees varies each term with the speaker's organization. For example, there were twenty-seven such committees in the assembly during 2001–2002, down from twenty-nine in 1999–2000. Some committees are far more important than others, so the speaker's friendship is of great value to a legislator. The speaker also carries favor with the governor, especially if the two work well together. The results can be stunning, as in 2000 when then-Speaker Bob Hertzberg requested $38 million in state budget "special project" funds for his district–13 percent of the entire legislature's request–and received virtually everything he sought.

By tradition, the party with a majority in the assembly chooses the speaker in a closed meeting, or caucus. A vote is then taken by the full assembly, with the choice already known to all. The minority party selects its leader in a similar fashion. Majority and minority floor leaders, as well as their whips (assistants), provide further support for the legislative officers. With solid majorities almost consistently since 1959 (Table 5.1), the Democrats have controlled the speakership for all but four years during the past four decades.

The last dominant speaker, Democrat Willie Brown of San Francisco, held the position from 1980 until 1995–a record. But term limits and a national tide in 1994 swept the Republicans back into power and, ultimately, the speakership. Republican rule lasted through 1996, when the Democrats captured a majority and selected Cruz Bustamante of Fresno as the assembly's first Latino speaker. This time, term limits, not legislative turnover, dictated the length of his stay. With Bustamante ineligible for reelection in 1998, the Democratic majority selected Antonio Villaraigosa of Los Angeles as the assembly leader, returning power to Southern California for the first time since 1974. Southern California's dominance has continued ever since, with the election of Bob Hertzberg in 2000 and Herb Wesson in 2001. Both selections were necessitated by term limits.

The senate has emphasized collegiality and cooperation over strong leadership, strict rules, and tight organization. However, both the senate hierarchy and key committees have assumed more partisan overtones over the past two decades. The most powerful member is the **president pro tem,** who, like the speaker, is elected by the majority party after

TABLE 5.1
POLITICAL PARTIES IN THE STATE LEGISLATURE, 1975–2004

LEGISLATIVE SESSION	SENATE			ASSEMBLY	
	DEMOCRATS	REPUBLICANS	INDEPENDENTS	DEMOCRATS	REPUBLICANS
1975–1976	25	15		55	25
1977–1978	26	14		57	23
1979–1980	25	15		50	30
1981–1982	23	17		48	32
1983–1984	25	14	1	48	32
1985–1986	25	15		47	33
1987–1988	24	15	1	44	36
1989–1990	24	15	1	47	33
1991–1992	27	12	2	47	33
1993–1994	23	15	2	49	31
1995–1996	21	17	2	39	41
1997–1998	22	17	1	42	38
1999–2000	25	15		48	32
2001–2002	26	14		50	30
2003–2004	26	14		48	32

each general election. The minority party also elects its leader then. The key to senate power lies within the five-member **Rules Committee,** which, chaired by the president pro tem, controls all other committee assignments and the flow of legislation. In 2001–2002 the senate had twenty-five standing committees, one more than in 1999–2000.

Senate partisanship increased in 1980, when Los Angeles Democrat David Roberti was chosen president pro tem. After consolidating control of the Rules Committee, Roberti doubled the size of the office staff with new policy-oriented aides; he also used his office to raise and dispense large sums to grateful fellow Democrats. In the process, Roberti made the president pro tem post more like that of the assembly speaker. Term limits forced Roberti to step down in 1994. He was replaced by fellow Democrat Bill Lockyer of Hayward, one of the last pre–Proposition 140 legislators, until term limits forced him to move on in 1998. Democrat John Burton of San Francisco, previously an assembly member for nearly twenty years, replaced Lockyer. Although a senator since only 1997, Burton's experience thwarts the turnover intentions of term limits. Many observers view him as the legislature's most formidable leader, despite the assembly speaker's traditionally dominant role.

STAFFING THE PROFESSIONAL LEGISLATURE

The evolution of the legislature into a full-time body was accompanied by a major expansion of its support staff. In 1990 the number of legislative assistants totaled 2,400–a far cry from the 485 employed by the last part-time legislature in 1966. Reductions from Proposition 140 pared the number of staffers to about 1,750, although increases in the state's population have led to a slow increase in the number of positions. Today about 2,500 staffers work for the legislature. Those in the capital usually concentrate on pending legislation, whereas district staffers spend much of their time on constituents' problems. The efforts of these staffers help each legislator to remain in good standing with his or her district.

Legislators spend much of their time in committees, the heart of the legislative process. Most committees cover specialized policy areas, such as education or natural resources. A few, such as the Senate and Assembly Rules Committees, deal with procedures and internal organization. Each committee employs staff consultants who are both experts on the committee's subject area and politically astute individuals–important attributes because they serve at the pleasure of the committee chair. Besides the traditional committees, staffers assist some eighty-four select committees (thirty-two in the Senate and fifty-two in the Assembly, as of 2002) and eleven joint committees that research narrow issues, coordinate two-house policy efforts, or oversee previously enacted legislation.

Another staff group is even more political. Employed by the Democratic and Republican caucuses and answering to the party leaders in the senate and assembly, these assistants are supposed to deal with possible legislation. However, their real activities usually center on advancing the interests of their party.

In addition to personal, committee, and leadership staffers, legislators have created neutral support agencies. With a staff of forty-nine, the **legislative analyst** (a position created in 1941) provides fiscal expertise, reviewing the annual budget and assessing programs that affect the state's coffers. The **legislative counsel** (a position created in 1913) employs about eighty-five attorneys to draft bills for legislators and to determine their potential impact on existing legislation. The **state auditor** (a position created in 1955) assists the legislature by periodically reviewing ongoing programs.

Historically, staffing has enhanced the legislature's professionalism. Yet some staffers, especially those who work for the legislative leaders, clearly spend more time on partisan politics than on legislation. Many have used their positions as apprenticeships to gain knowledge, skills, and contacts for their own campaign efforts. Like many of his colleagues, Herb Wesson, the current assembly speaker, began his career as a staffer. All this, critics point out, is funded by the taxpayers. Defenders of the system counter that this staffing system helps compensate for weak party organizations.

The total budget for legislative operations in 1990–1991 was $165 million, compared with $73 million for 1979–1980. But the passage of Proposition 140 in 1990 reversed the legislature's growth and greatly reduced its operating budget. Within three months of its passage, the legislature was forced to pare its 1991–1992 budget to $114 million. By the 2002–2003 fiscal year, the legislature's budget climbed to $201 million. However, the larger numbers were driven by a growing population and inflation, rather than dramatically expanded state services.

HOW A BILL BECOMES A LAW

The legislature passes laws; it also proposes constitutional amendments, which may be submitted for voter approval after they receive absolute two-thirds majority votes in both houses (the votes of two-thirds of the full membership—that is, twenty-seven votes in the senate and fifty-four in the assembly). The same absolute two-thirds majority votes are required for the legislature to offer bond measures—money borrowed for long-term, expensive state projects. Proposed bond measures must then obtain majority votes at the next election before becoming law.

Most of the legislature's energy, however, is spent on lawmaking. Absolute majorities—twenty-one votes in the senate, forty-one votes in the assembly—are required to pass basic laws intended to take effect the following January, but absolute two-thirds votes in both houses are required for appropriations, urgency measures (those that become law immediately upon the governor's signature), and overrides of the governor's veto. The process, however, is far from simple.

THE FORMAL PROCESS

The legislative process begins when the assembly member or senator sponsoring a bill gives the clerk of the chamber a copy, which is recorded and numbered (Figure 5.2). The bill then undergoes three readings and several hearings before it is sent to the other house for a repeat of the process. The first reading simply acknowledges the bill's submission. Typically, a bill is assigned to two or three committees for careful scrutiny by members who are experts in that bill's subject area.

Depending on the bill's origin, either the Senate Rules Committee or the Assembly Rules Committee decides on the route of the bill. The chairs of these important committees can also affect a bill's fate by sending it to "friendly" or "hostile" committees and by assigning it a favorable or unfavorable route. More than half of all bills die in committee.

More than 6,000 bills are introduced during each two-year session, with assembly members limited to 50 and senators limited to 65 proposals. With such volume, legislative committees are essential to getting laws passed. They hold hearings, debate, and eventually vote on each bill delegated to them. Most committees deal in narrow areas, but a few, such as the Senate Finance Committee and the Assembly Ways and Means Committee, focus on the collection and distribution of funds and thus enjoy clout that goes beyond any one policy area.

At the conclusion of its hearings, a committee can kill a bill, release it without recommendation, or approve it with a "do pass" proposal. It may also recommend approval contingent upon certain changes or amendments. Only when a bill receives a positive recommendation from all of the committees in a house is it likely to get a second reading by the full legislative body. At this stage, the house considers additional amendments. After all proposed revisions have been discussed, the bill is printed in its final form and presented to the full house for a third reading. After further debate on the entire bill, a vote is taken.

If approved, the bill goes to the other house, where the process starts anew. Again, the bill may die anywhere along the perilous legislative path. Should the two houses pass different versions of the same bill, the versions must be reconciled by a **conference committee.** Senate members are appointed by the Rules Committee; assembly members are chosen by the speaker. If the conference committee agrees on a single version and if both houses approve it by the required margins, the bill goes to the governor for his or her approval. Otherwise, the proposed legislation is dead.

Usually, a bill becomes law if the governor signs it or takes no action within twelve days. However, if it has been passed immediately before a session's end, the governor has thirty days to act. If the governor vetoes the bill, an absolute two-thirds majority must be attained in both houses for it to become law. Attaining such a lopsided vote is next to impossible, so vetoed bills generally fall by the wayside.

THE INFORMAL PROCESS

Politics penetrates the formal, "textbook" process by which a bill becomes law. This means that every piece of legislation is considered not only on its merits but also on the basis of political support, interest group pressure, public opinion, and personal power.

Partisanship has become more pronounced since the late 1950s, with members of the majority party chairing most, if not all, of the committees in any given year. With Democrats in control for most of the past three decades, they have reaped the benefits of the committee chairs (extra staff, procedural advantages, and so forth) and secured the best committee assignments. Likewise, when assembly Republicans briefly held a bare majority in 1996, they assumed control of twenty-five of the twenty-six committees.

Public opinion also affects legislation, sometimes dramatically. Recent statutes on excessive drinking, smoke-free restaurants and bars, assault weapons, and longer sentences for repeat felon offenders have been enacted in direct response to public concern.

Political support within the legislature is essential to numerous decisions. So many bills flow through the process that members often vote on measures they haven't even read, relying on staff, committee, or leadership recommendations. Sometimes, a bill's fate may also rest with key legislative leaders, who can use their positions to stifle or speed up a proposal at various points in the legislative process. Outcomes are also affected by **logrolling,** a give-and-take bargaining process in which legislators agree to support each other's bills. More often than not, legislators give away their votes on matters of little concern to them in hopes of mollifying opponents or pleasing powerful leaders.

As noted in Chapter 4, interest group pressure permeates the legislative process. With the combined cost of legislative campaigns leaping from $7 million in 1966 to $86.6 million in 1998, candidates have welcomed contributions and, in some cases, accepted them illegally. The assembly speaker and senate president pro tem have become the primary recipients of interest group contributions, directing those dollars, in turn, to key legislative races. Although this practice has enhanced

FIGURE 5.2
HOW A BILL BECOMES A LAW

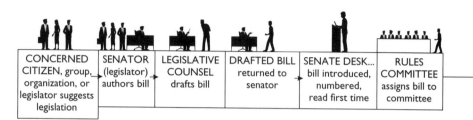

| CONCERNED CITIZEN, group, organization, or legislator suggests legislation | SENATOR (legislator) authors bill | LEGISLATIVE COUNSEL drafts bill | DRAFTED BILL returned to senator | SENATE DESK... bill introduced, numbered, read first time | RULES COMMITTEE assigns bill to committee |

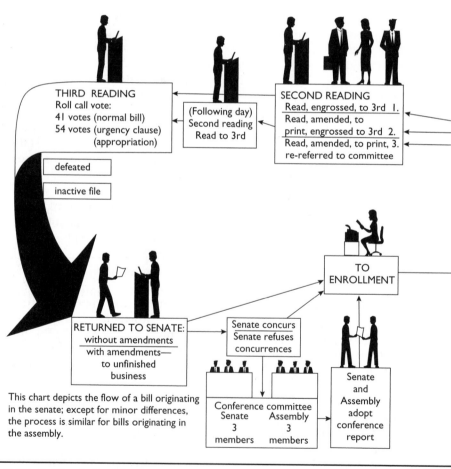

THIRD READING
Roll call vote:
41 votes (normal bill)
54 votes (urgency clause)
        (appropriation)

defeated

inactive file

(Following day)
Second reading
Read to 3rd

SECOND READING
Read, engrossed, to 3rd 1.
Read, amended, to print, engrossed to 3rd 2.
Read, amended, to print, 3.
re-referred to committee

RETURNED TO SENATE:
without amendments
with amendments—
to unfinished business

Senate concurs
Senate refuses concurrences

TO ENROLLMENT

Conference committee
Senate   Assembly
   3   3
members   members

Senate and Assembly adopt conference report

This chart depicts the flow of a bill originating in the senate; except for minor differences, the process is similar for bills originating in the assembly.

SOURCE: California Legislature.

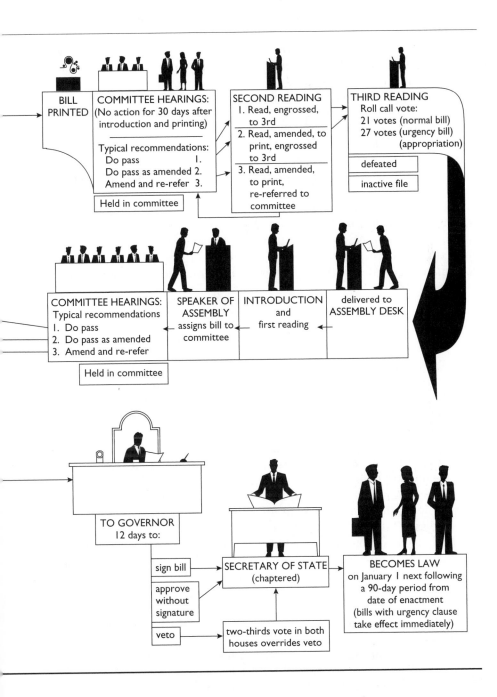

BILL PRINTED

COMMITTEE HEARINGS: (No action for 30 days after introduction and printing)

Typical recommendations:
Do pass   1.
Do pass as amended 2.
Amend and re-refer 3.

Held in committee

SECOND READING
1. Read, engrossed, to 3rd
2. Read, amended, to print, engrossed to 3rd
3. Read, amended, to print, re-referred to committee

THIRD READING
Roll call vote:
21 votes (normal bill)
27 votes (urgency bill) (appropriation)

defeated

inactive file

COMMITTEE HEARINGS:
Typical recommendations
1. Do pass
2. Do pass as amended
3. Amend and re-refer

Held in committee

SPEAKER OF ASSEMBLY assigns bill to committee

INTRODUCTION and first reading

delivered to **ASSEMBLY DESK**

TO GOVERNOR 12 days to:

sign bill

approve without signature

veto

SECRETARY OF STATE (chaptered)

two-thirds vote in both houses overrides veto

BECOMES LAW on January 1 next following a 90-day period from date of enactment (bills with urgency clause take effect immediately) their power over legislators, it has not reduced the role of money in campaigns. In fact, the flow has been astounding; Senate President Pro Tem John Burton received nearly $10 million in 1998, easily eclipsing all previous records. Then-Assembly Speaker Antonio Villaraigosa also raised $8.2 million during the same year. In these and other instances, well-positioned legislators have used their contributions to help the campaigns of their legislative allies.

Finally, personal power within the legislature remains a component of the political process, especially in cases of conflict. One such example occurred in 2000, when Senate President Pro Tem John Burton used his power to block Governor Davis's reappointment of the chair of Board of Prison Terms after the governor appealed a court decision that upheld special care for disabled prisoners.[8] This occurred despite the fact that Davis and Burton both belong to the Democratic party.

Repeatedly, various interest and citizen groups have managed and secured approval of initiatives designed to pare the ability of collecting and spending campaign funds. In virtually each case, however, courts have struck down such efforts as violations of the freedom of speech guarantee associated with the First Amendment in the U.S. Constitution.

UNFINISHED BUSINESS

Today's legislature faces myriad issues, ranging from a questionable public education system to a deteriorating infrastructure. Faced with revolving participants, the legislature operates with little stability and less tradition. Handcuffed by term limits, restrictions on budget growth (see Chapter 8), and recession for most of the past decade, the legislature has struggled to maintain the status quo in most policy areas.

With all these pressures, legislators often seem to react to problems rather than to anticipate or solve them. As a consequence, public policies are made increasingly by initiative, the governor, or the courts. Nevertheless, the legislature continues to grapple with leading issues of the day and, at least sometimes, lawmakers are able to overcome assorted obstacles to enact policies of substance.

Notes

1. "Confidence Is Up, But Politicians' Popularity Is Not," *Los Angeles Times,* March 22, 1996, pp. A1, A22.
2. "High Approval Rating of State Legislature. Term Limits Still Heavily Favored," The Field Poll, Release 1921, April 8, 1999, p. 2.
3. The Field Poll, Release 2029, February 7, 2002, p. 7.

4. In general, the plan provided one senator per county. In a few cases, two small counties shared a senator, and in one case, three very small counties–Alpine, Inyo, and Mono–shared a senator.

5. Legislators also receive tax-free daily expense stipends; monthly allowances for cars (including gasoline and maintenance); life, health, dental, vision, and disability insurance; and funds to travel between their districts and the capital.

6. Kathleen Les, "Mr. Mayor Goes to the Capitol," *California Journal* (Vol. XXX, No. 10, October 1999), pp. 36–38.

7. See "Assembly's Profile Little Changed by Term Limits." *Los Angeles Times,* December 2, 1996, pp. A1, A22.

8. See "Senate Chief Blocks Davis Selection," *Los Angeles Times,* March 10, 2000, pp. A3, A23.

Learn More on the World Wide Web

About the California Legislature:
Legislative Analyst's Office: www.lao.ca.gov
State Assembly: www.assembly.ca.gov
State Senate: www.senate.ca.gov

About state legislatures:
www.ncsl.org

Learn More at the Library

Bruce E. Cain and Roger G. Noll, eds., *Constitutional Reform in California,* Berkeley: Institute of Governmental Studies Press, University of California, 1995.

2001–2002 California Political Almanac, 7th edition, California Journal.

Alan Rosenthal, *The Decline of Representative Democracy: Process, Participation and Power in State Legislatures,* Washington, DC: Congressional Quarterly Press, 1998.

See also . . .

The *California Channel* on most cable systems. Watch the legislature at work!

Chapter 6

COURTS, JUDGES, AND POLITICS: CALIFORNIA LAW

Courts are very much a part of the political process. Judges and politicians have always known this, but the public has been slower to understand the political nature of the judiciary. When governors made a few controversial appointments to the courts during the 1970s and 1980s, however, judicial politics became a very public matter. Recently, judicial politics has become apparent in court decisions overturning popular initiatives.

What makes the courts political? Not just controversial judicial decisions or even the involvement of party politicians. Courts are political because their judgments are choices between public policy alternatives. When judges consider cases, they evaluate the issues before them both in terms of existing legislation and in the context of the U.S. and state constitutions. Differing judicial interpretations of these documents help some people and hurt others. This is why the courts, like members of the executive and legislature branches, are subject to the attentions and pressures of California's competing interests, and this is why the courts are political.

THE CALIFORNIA COURT SYSTEM

The California court system has three levels; each has its own responsibilities, but all are linked. Most cases begin and end at the lowest level. Only a few move up the state's judicial ladder through the appeals process (Figure 6.1). Under certain circumstances, a few state cases may end in the U.S. Supreme Court.

THE JUDICIAL LADDER

The vast majority of cases begin and end in **trial courts,** the bottom rung of the judicial ladder. Cases were once divided between municipal and superior courts according to how serious they were, but in 1998,

FIGURE 6.1

The California Court System

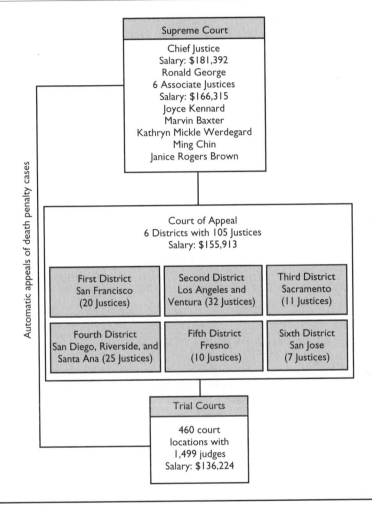

SOURCE: California Judicial Council.

voters approved an initiative constitutional amendment allowing counties to merge their courts, so now a single court system in each county
handles misdemeanor cases (minor crimes, including most traffic
offenses), felonies (serious crimes subject to sentences of one year or
more in state prison), civil suits (noncriminal disputes), divorces, and
juvenile cases. Each county also operates small claims courts–special

offices that allow an individual to take a case with damage claims up to $2,500 before a judge without the presence of attorneys—sort of like TV's *Judge Judy.*

Losers in trial courts may ask the court on the next rung of the judicial ladder to review the decision. Most cases aren't appealed, but when major crimes and penalties or big money are involved, the losers in the cases sometimes request a review by one of California's six district **courts of appeal.** As appellate bodies, these courts do not hold trials like the ones we see on television. Lawyers make arguments and submit briefs to panels of three justices that try to determine whether the original trial was fairly conducted. If they decide it was not, they can send the case back for another trial or even dismiss the charges.

Ultimately, parties to the cases may petition for review by the seven-member state **supreme court,** the top of California's judicial ladder. Few cases reach this level because most are resolved in the lower courts and the high court declines most petitions. If a case reaches the California Supreme Court, its decision is final unless issues of federal law or the U.S. Constitution arise; the U.S. Supreme Court may consider such cases.

If a higher court refuses an appeal, the lower court's decision stands. Even when a case is accepted, the justices of the higher court have agreed only to consider the issues. They may or may not overturn the decision of the lower court.

JUDICIAL ELECTION AND SELECTION

Although the tiered structure of the California courts is similar to that of the federal courts, the selection of judges is not. Federal judges and members of the U.S. Supreme Court are appointed by the president and confirmed by the U.S. Senate, and they serve for life. California judges and justices, however, gain office through a more complicated process and regularly face the voters. This periodic scrutiny by the public, media, and interest groups helps keep judges and their decisions in the news.

Formal qualifications to become a judge are few: Candidates must have been admitted to practice law in California for a minimum number of five years. Technically these judges are elected, but most actually gain office through appointment by the governor when a judge dies, retires, or is promoted between elections. Appointed judges must run for office when the terms of the judges they replace expire, but running as incumbents, they almost always win. Trial court judges can also gain office simply by declaring their candidacy for a specific judicial office and running. If no candidate wins a majority in the primary election, the two with the most votes face each other in a **runoff election** in November. They serve a six-year term and then may run for reelection.

APPOINTMENTS AND THE HIGHER COURTS

Unlike lower court judges, members of the district courts of appeal and the state supreme court attain office only through gubernatorial appointment. The governor's possible nominees are first screened by the state's legal community through its Commission on Judicial Nominees Evaluation. Then the nominees must be approved by the **Commission on Judicial Appointments,** a three-member group consisting of the attorney general, the chief justice of the state supreme court, and the senior presiding judge of the courts of appeal. The commission may reject a nominee, but it has done so only twice since its creation in 1934.

Once approved by the Commission on Judicial Appointments, the new justices take office, but they must go before the voters at the next gubernatorial election. No opponents appear on the ballot; the voters simply check "yes" or "no" on the retention of the justices in question. If approved, they serve the remainder of the twelve-year term of the person they have replaced, at which time they can seek voter confirmation for a standard twelve-year term and additional terms after that.

A dozen other states select their supreme court justices in a similar fashion, but twenty-six rely solely on elections. The governor or legislature appoints justices in the remaining twelve states.

FIRING JUDGES

Almost all judges are easily elected and reelected, mostly without opposition. Those who designed the system probably intended this. They wanted to distance judges somewhat from politics and to ensure their independence by giving them relatively long terms, thus also ensuring relatively consistent interpretation of the law. Avoiding costly election campaigns that depend on financial contributors also promotes independence. The framers of the U.S. Constitution put such a high value on judicial continuity and independence that they provided for selection by appointment rather than by election and allowed judges to serve for life. For most of California's history, these values also seemed well entrenched in its political culture, and the state's judges functioned without much criticism or interference. Nevertheless, the California constitution provides several mechanisms of judicial accountability, all of which have been used recently. Judges may be removed through elections, but they may also be reprimanded or removed by the judicial system itself.

Incumbent justices of the California Supreme Court routinely won reelection without serious challenge until 1966, when a backlash against the civil rights movement led to an unsuccessful campaign to unseat justices who were viewed as too liberal. A few years later, several lower court judges appointed by Governor Jerry Brown during the 1970s faced challenges because critics viewed them as lenient toward criminals. In 1980, one-third of the trial court judges up for election were either defeated or forced into runoff elections. Women and minority judges were most likely to be challenged and to lose.

Although early efforts to oust liberal members of the state supreme court failed, anticourt elements triumphed in 1986, when Chief Justice Rose Bird and two other liberal justices appointed by Brown were swept out of office. Since then, the anticourt fervor has subsided. Today sitting judges are rarely challenged.

Judges can also be removed by the judicial system itself. The **Commission on Judicial Performance** was created in 1960 to investigate charges of misconduct or incompetence. Its members include three judges (appointed by the supreme court), two lawyers (appointed by the governor), and six public members (two each appointed by the governor, the Senate Rules Committee, and the speaker of the assembly). Few investigations result in any action, but if the charges are confirmed, the commission may impose censure, removal from office, or forced retirement.

Hundreds of complaints against judges are filed with the commission each year; about one-third are investigated. In rare cases when the commission finds a judge to be at fault, it usually issues a warning. Even more rarely, the commission may remove a judge from the bench. In a recent scandal in San Diego, several judges were admonished for accepting gifts from attorneys who appeared before them. One of their colleagues was removed from office and two others resigned while under investigation. Two were eventually sentenced to prison. Actual removal from the bench is extremely rare because, like the San Diego judges, those whose conduct is questionable usually resign before the commission's investigation is completed.

THE COURTS AT WORK

In 2000–2001, 8.1 million cases were filed in California's trial courts. Most of these were criminal cases. About 1.5 million were civil suits on such matters as divorce or contract disputes. Some observers think this volume of cases is a result of the eagerness of Californians to resolve issues in the courts, spurred on by more than 140,000 attorneys working in California. But a 1995 study found that, on a per capita basis, California's rate of civil disputes is below the national average.[1]

California's constitution guarantees the right to a jury trial for both criminal and civil cases; if both parties agree, however, a judge alone may hear the case. Jurors are drawn from lists of licensed drivers, voters, and property owners, but finding a twelve-member jury is often difficult. Many people avoid jury duty because it takes time away from work and pays only a few dollars a day. Homemakers and retired people are most readily available, but they alone cannot make up a balanced jury. Poor people and minorities tend to be underrepresented because they are less likely to be on the lists from which jurors are drawn; some avoid participation in a system they distrust.

The parties in civil cases provide their own lawyers, although legal aid societies sometimes help those who can't afford counsel. In criminal cases, the **district attorney,** an elected county official, carries out the prosecution. Defendants hire their own attorneys or are provided with a court-appointed attorney if they cannot afford one. California's larger counties have a **public defender** to provide such assistance. Well over half of all felony defendants require court-appointed help.

Most cases never go to trial, however. Nearly 90 percent of all criminal cases are resolved by **plea bargaining,** which results in a pretrial agreement on a plea and a penalty. Plea bargaining reduces the heavy workload of the courts and guarantees some punishment or restitution, but it also allows those charged with a crime to serve shorter sentences than they might have received if convicted of all charges. The majority of all civil suits are also settled without a trial when the parties to the cases reach an agreement to avoid the high costs and long delays of a trial.[2] Less than 1 percent of all cases are tried before a jury; a judge alone hears the rest.

Significantly, the judicial system as a whole–from judges to prosecutors, public defenders, lawyers, and juries–does not reflect the diversity of California's people. Only 17 percent of California's attorneys are non-white. A Judicial Council study reports that more than 80 percent of all judges, prosecuting attorneys, public defenders, and other court officials are white, while a substantial majority of defendants are not. The study also expressed concern about evidence that punishment is less severe for whites than for minorities convicted of the same crime. African Americans, and to a lesser extent other minorities, perceive this and express deep mistrust of the system.[3]

APPEALS

When a dispute arises over a trial proceeding or its outcome, the losing party may appeal to a higher court to review the case. Most appeals are refused, but the higher courts may agree to hear a case because of previous procedural problems (for instance, if the defendant was not read his or her rights) or because it raises untested legal issues. Appellate courts do not retry the case or review the facts in evidence; their job is to see that the trial was fair and that the law was appropriately applied. In addition to traditional appellate cases, the state supreme court also automatically reviews all death penalty decisions. Although few in number, these cases take up a substantial amount of the court's time. A few other cases come to it directly. Known as "original proceedings," these include cases involving writs of mandamus (ordering a government action) and habeas corpus (a request for reasons why someone is in custody). Neither the courts of appeal nor the state supreme court can initiate cases. No matter how eager they are to intervene in an issue, they have to wait for someone else to bring the case to them.

Every year about 9,000 petitions are filed with the California Supreme Court, mostly requesting reviews of cases decided by the courts of appeal. Meeting in conference on Wednesdays, each year the members of the court choose about 200 petitions for consideration, a task that consumes an estimated 40 percent of the court's time. By refusing to hear a case, the court allows the preceding decision to stand. When the court grants a hearing, one of the justices (or a staff member) writes a "calendar" memo analyzing the case. Attorneys representing the two sides present written briefs and then oral arguments, during which they may face rigorous questioning by the justices.

After hearing the oral arguments, the justices discuss the case in conference and vote in order of seniority; the chief justice casts the final, sometimes decisive, vote. If the chief justice agrees with the majority, he or she can assign a justice to write the official court opinion; usually this is the same justice who wrote the initial calendar memo. A draft of the opinion then circulates among the justices, each of whom may concur, suggest changes, or write a dissenting opinion. Finally, after many months, the court's decision is made public. The court issued 103 opinions in 2000–2001–about 1 percent of all the cases filed.

This time-consuming process allows plenty of room for politicking among the justices and depends on a high degree of cooperation and deferential behavior among justices–what judges call **"collegiality"**–as a way of building consensus on issues before the court. With seven independent minds on the court, ongoing negotiations are needed to reach a majority and a decision.

RUNNING THE COURTS

In addition to deciding cases, the chief justice acts as the administrative head of the California court system. This entails setting procedures for hearings and deliberations, managing public information for the supreme court, and overseeing its staff. The chief justice also assigns cases to specific appellate courts and appoints temporary justices when there are vacancies on the supreme court because of disqualification, illness, or retirement.

As chair of the **Judicial Council,** the chief justice also takes a hand in managing the entire state court system. The Judicial Council has twenty-one members, including one associate justice (appointed by the chief justice), three appellate court judges, and ten lower court judges. Also on the council are four attorneys (appointed by the state bar association), plus one state senator and one assembly member appointed by their respective legislative houses. The Judicial Council makes the rules for court procedures, collects data on the operations and workload of the courts, and gives seminars for judges.

Recent chief justices have exhibited very different styles as managers of the state court system. Chief Justice Rose Bird (1977–1987), a liberal appointed by Governor Jerry Brown, tried to shake up the system and made herself unpopular with the state's legal establishment. The legal profession and the media view Ronald George, the current chief justice, more favorably. Personable and accessible, Chief Justice George has been credited with reinvigorating the courts and their image.

THE HIGH COURT AS A POLITICAL BATTLEGROUND

The courts are particularly important and powerful in California because of the nature of California government and politics. California's constitution is long and elaborately specific, dealing with all sorts of matters, both major and mundane; its index alone is twice as long as the entire U.S. Constitution. The complexity of California's constitution is reflected in the government it lays out and is increased through constant revision by initiative. In turn, the length, detail, and continually changing complexity of California's constitution give its courts greater power because they have the job of determining whether laws and public policy are consistent with the constitution. One scholar has called the courts a "shadow government"[4] because of their increasing importance in shaping public policy, but others view this as their appropriate constitutional role.

At the top of California's judicial ladder is the state supreme court, the ultimate interpreter of the state constitution (unless issues arise under the U.S. Constitution). The court's power makes it a center of political interest: Governors strive to appoint justices who share their values and pay close attention to the appointment process. A governor who is elected to two terms of office may have appointed as many as half the state's sitting judges, significantly affecting judicial practices. As governors have changed, so have the sorts of justices they appoint (Table 6.1). And as its membership has changed, the California Supreme Court has moved across the spectrum from liberal to conservative.

Regardless of their collective political values, the court has not backed away from controversial issues, including occasionally overturning decisions by the legislature or the people (as expressed in initiatives). This is less because of interventionist attitudes on the part of the justices than because of a long, complex, and frequently amended constitution and poorly written laws and initiatives.

TABLE 6.1
JUDICIAL APPOINTMENTS BY CALIFORNIA GOVERNORS, 1959–2002

	MALE	FEMALE	WHITE	BLACK	HISPANIC	ASIAN
Edmund G. Brown, Sr.	97.7%	2.3%	93.0%	3.0%	2.5%	1.5%
1959–1967	(390)	(10)	(372)	(12)	(10)	(6)
Ronald Reagan	97.4	2.6	93.1	2.6	3.3	1.0
1967–1975	(478)	(13)	(457)	(13)	(16)	(5)
Jerry Brown	84.0	16.0	75.5	10.9	9.4	4.3
1975–1983	(691)	(132)	(621)	(90)	(77)	(35)
George Deukmejian	84.8	15.2	87.7	3.6	5.0	3.6
1983–1991	(821)	(147)	(849)	(35)	(49)	(35)
Pete Wilson	74.6	25.4	84.4	5.2	4.9	5.5
1991–1998	(517)	(176)	(585)	(36)	(34)	(38)
Gray Davis	66.4	33.6	70.2	12.5	9.5	7.8
1999–2002	(154)	(78)	(163)	(29)	(22)	(18)

SOURCE: Governor's Office.

GOVERNORS, VOTERS, AND THE COURTS

Long dominated by liberals, California's supreme court took a distinct turn to the right in 1986, when the voters rejected Chief Justice Rose Bird and two liberal associate justices. Appointed in 1977 by Governor Jerry Brown, Bird was California's first woman justice. She was a controversial choice because of her liberalism, her lack of experience as a judge, and her age, which, at forty, was considered young for such a high post.

Bird joined a liberal majority on the court and was soon criticized for being too sympathetic to criminal defendants, favoring busing as a means of school desegregation, and opposing Proposition 13, the immensely popular property-tax reduction initiative. The voters confirmed Bird's appointment in 1978 by 51.7 percent, the lowest ever in the history of California's judicial elections. Despite her close call, the chief justice and the liberal court majority continued to hand down controversial decisions. Even as public concern about crime increased, for example, they consistently reversed death sentences on what critics viewed as legal technicalities. When the justices were on the ballot in 1986, voters rejected Bird and two other Brown-appointed justices while confirming a less controversial Democrat and two new conservatives appointed by Brown's successor, Republican George Deukmejian. Soon thereafter, Governor Deukmejian transformed the court with conservative appointees, including promoting Malcolm Lucas, an earlier appointee, to chief justice.

Subsequent appointees by Republican Governor Pete Wilson maintained the court's conservative majority. Led by Chief Justice Ronald M. George, today's court includes Deukmejian appointees Marvin Baxter and Joyce Kennard and Wilson appointees Kathryn Werdegar, Ming Chin, and Janice Rogers Brown. Carlos Moreno, the court's only Democrat, was appointed by Governor Davis in 2001. Minority members of the court include Moreno (Latino), Brown (African American), Chin (Chinese), and Kennard (Dutch-Indonesian). But as Table 6.1 suggests, women and minorities are underrepresented in the California judiciary as a whole.

Since Bird's rejection, justices have won voter approval with 56 to 76 percent voting for retention. The chief justice and Justices Brown, Chin, and Mosk were on the ballot in November 1998. Antiabortion forces targeted Chin and George because of their controversial 1997 votes to reverse a previous court decision requiring minors to obtain parental consent for abortions. The worried justices raised $1.6 million for their campaigns, hired consultants, and met with the editorial boards of the state's major newspapers. In the end all four justices won retention, with 69 to 76 percent voting in their favor.

Governor Gray Davis, a Democrat elected in 1998, has had the opportunity to name only one justice to the supreme court–Carlos Moreno, the third Latino to serve on the court. His appointments to lower courts have been more diverse than those of his predecessor, but he has made it clear that he will appoint only judges who agree with him, especially in being tough on crime. "My appointees should reflect my views," he declared, although he later said, "I fully respect the independence of the judiciary as a coequal branch of government."[5] Legal experts and political leaders objected to Davis's expectation that his appointees would carry out his agenda, but previous governors have expected the same of those they name to the bench. Once appointed, however, judges often assert their independence.

THE COURTS, THE VOTERS, AND THE CONSTITUTION

With a Republican-appointed majority since 1986, the once-liberal supreme court has become solidly conservative, tending to be pro-prosecution in criminal cases and pro-business in economic cases. But the court has maintained its independence as the third branch of state government, and its impact on state politics remains significant.

Although labeled pro-business, the court upheld a 1988 initiative that regulated the powerful insurance industry. Consumer advocates were frustrated, however, by the fact that the court took nearly six years to hold a hearing on the crucial rate-rollback provisions of the proposition. The court also disappointed local governments seeking new taxes with 1991 and 1996 rulings that rigidly applied a requirement for two-thirds voter approval in accordance with 1978's Proposition 13 (see Chapter 8).

The court has demonstrated independence in other areas as well. For example, it has followed the Bird court's precedent of approving state-funded abortions, and in 1995 the "conservative" court surprised some observers with a ruling that banned sex discrimination at a private country club. The court also handed Republican Governor Pete Wilson a defeat in 1997 when it ruled against his plan to privatize the work of the state transportation agency.

More controversially, the courts sometimes overrule decisions of the voters. In 1999, for example, the California Supreme Court struck down a voter-approved initiative statute (or law) allowing gambling on Indian reservations because it conflicted with the state constitution. Proponents put the issue back on the ballot in 2000 as a constitutional amendment, again winning voter approval. Again displaying their independence, the Republican-dominated court removed a Republican-sponsored initiative on reapportionment from the March 2000 ballot because it included issues other than reapportionment and the state constitution limits initiatives to a single subject. Initiatives have been removed from the ballot only five times before.

Sometimes the federal courts join the fray. In 1995, for example, a federal judge declared portions of Proposition 187–an initiative that limited public services to immigrants–unconstitutional on grounds that only the federal government has authority over immigration. In 2000 the U.S. Supreme Court rejected California's voter-approved blanket or "open" primary on grounds that it violated the rights of free speech and association of political parties. The federal courts have also overturned a series of initiatives on campaign finance, ruling that the contribution limits set by these measures were unconstitutional.

Although these rulings against voter-approved laws appear undemocratic, the state and federal courts were doing their duty to interpret these controversial propositions not only for their contents but for their consistency with the state and national constitutionals. When the courts find an act of another branch of government or of the voters to be contrary to existing law or to the state or federal constitution, it is their responsibility to overturn that law, even if their decision is unpopular. "Periodically, cyclically," said Chief Justice George, "the courts have to exercise their function in a way that brings them into direct collision with the other branches of government and possibly with the public will."[6]

COURTS AND THE POLITICS OF CRIME

Crime topped the list of voter concerns in California and the nation for most of the past two decades. Murder, rape, burglary, gang wars, and random violence seemed all too common. A 1994 Field Poll found that 53 percent of all Californians were either "very" or "somewhat" fearful of being victimized by serious crime, up from 42 percent in 1992.[7] Republicans George Deukmejian and Pete Wilson were elected governor at least partly because they were seen as law-and-order candidates.

Capital punishment was a key issue in the 1980s, when Chief Justice Rose Bird and her liberal colleagues on the supreme court overturned the vast majority of death penalty cases they reviewed. Egged on by Governor Deukmejian and others, the voters rejected these liberals in 1986. Since their removal, the supreme court has affirmed most death sentences. The issue has not quite gone away, however. Law-and-order advocates still condemn the lengthy delays in death penalty appeals–up to ten years for the state courts and another ten years for the federal courts. Execution is a serious business, and no one wants to make a mistake. Judges who are liberal or merely reluctant may cause some of the delay, but experts estimate that much is due to the inability of the courts to find legal counsel for the condemned. Meanwhile, public support for the death penalty has declined from 80 percent in 1992 to 63 percent in 2000. Forensic methods such as DNA testing have revealed wrongful convictions in death penalty cases so frequently that 73 percent of Californians now favor a moratorium on executions.[8]

Along with capital punishment, tougher sentences for other crimes were also seen as part of the solution. In 1982 voters passed **Proposition 8,** "The Victims' Bill of Rights," an initiative that strengthened penalties for many crimes. Then in 1994 the "three strikes" law was enacted by the legislature and, at the urging of Governor Wilson, by initiative. The new law reflected public concern about crime and the view that liberal judges who were "soft on crime" were letting criminals off with light sentences. Although the conservatism of the courts made this perception questionable, it was widely held and politically potent. **"Three strikes"** required that anyone convicted of three felonies serve a sentence of twenty-five years to life or, in other words, "three strikes and you're out."

The three strikes law quickly increased the state's prison population, and spending on prisons (see Chapter 8) also greatly increased. New prisons were built, and operating the state prison system absorbs an ever-growing share of the state budget. With many of the state's worst criminals incarcerated for life, three strikes prosecutions have declined, however. Currently, only 4 percent of the state prison population are three-strikes offenders.[9]

Meanwhile, California's crime rate has declined dramatically. Conservative leaders attribute this to tougher judges and penalties. A University of California study, however, found that "most of the decline in crime had nothing to do with three strikes" because the law applies to such a small percentage of cases.[10] Some experts argue that the declining crime rate is due to economic prosperity and demographics, with fewer people in the age group most commonly associated with criminal activity. In any case, crime had far less resonance as an issue in the 1998 and 2002 gubernatorial elections. The Republican candidates weren't able to use the issue to their advantage because voters had other concerns and because Democrat Gray Davis, the winner, supported capital punishment and promised to appoint judges who would be tough on crime.

On one key issue on crime, however, the approach of Governor Davis and his Democratic allies was different. In 1999 California led the nation in the enactment of gun control laws, including limits on buying handguns, stronger controls on assault weapons, requirements for trigger locks, and a ban on the manufacture of cheap handguns.

The debate continues, but as the crime rate declines, so does the political urgency of the issue. A 2002 opinion poll reported that only 3 percent of Californians rated crime as the issue they most wanted their gubernatorial candidates to talk about, whereas 17 percent picked education.[11]

POLITICS AND THE COURTS

Crime and other issues discussed in this chapter remind us that the courts play a central role in the politics of our state. Recent controversies about judicial appointments and decisions make the political nature of the courts apparent, yet the courts have never been free of politics. They are in the business of making policy and interpreting the law; their judgments vary with the values of those who make them.

Notes

1. *San Francisco Chronicle,* March 8, 1995, p. A21.
2. Judicial Council, *2000 Court Statistics Report.*
3. Judicial Council Advisory Committee Report on Racial and Ethnic Bias in the Courts, 1997.
4. Charles Price, "Shadow Government," *California Journal,* October 1997, p. 38.
5. *San Jose Mercury News,* February 1, 2000, p. 14A and February 2, 2000, p. 9B.
6. *Los Angeles Times,* July 24, 1996.

7. *California Opinion Index,* March 1994.

8. Theodore Hamm, "The Death Penalty," *California Journal,* August 2002, p. 9.

9. *San Jose Mercury News,* December 28, 2001.

10. Franklin E. Zimring, Sam Kamin, and Gordon Hawkins, *Crime and Punishment in California: The Impact of Three Strikes and You're Out,* Berkeley: Institute of Governmental Studies, 1999, p. 84.

11. Public Policy Institute of California, Statewide Survey, August 2002 (www.ppic.org).

Learn More on the World Wide Web

California's court system: www.courtinfo.ca.gov

State Bar of California: www.calbar.org

California Judges Association: www.calcourts.org

Learn More at the Library

Betty Medsger, *Framed: The New Right Attack on Chief Justice Rose Bird and the Courts,* New York: Pilgrim, 1983.

Preble Stolz, *Judging Judges: The Investigation of Rose Bird and the California Supreme Court,* New York: The Free Press, 1981.

Franklin E. Zimring, Sam Kamin, and Gordon Hawkins, *Crime and Punishment in California: The Impact of Three Strikes and You're Out,* Berkeley: Institute of Governmental Studies, 1999.

CHAPTER 7

THE EXECUTIVE BRANCH: COPING WITH FRAGMENTED AUTHORITY

■━━━━■

The **governor** is California's most powerful public official. He or she shapes the state budget, appoints key policymakers in the executive and judicial branches, participates in reapportionment of the legislature and California congressional delegation, and interacts with public opinion by taking positions on controversial issues. There are also times when the governor's powers extend even beyond his or her normally broad limits to occasional disasters such as California's massive power crisis in 2001.

Unlike the President of the United States, however, the governor of California shares authority with seven other independently elected executive officers. Occasionally, these other executives clash with the governor over the use of power, as do the legislature and the judiciary. In the past, such fragmentation of executive authority has accounted for occasional standoffs and public pandering. There has been one change in this dynamic, however. Term limits, although applicable to both the executive and legislative branches, have left the governor in a stronger position relative to the legislature because of the near-certainty of two four-year terms of office.

THE GOVERNOR: FIRST AMONG EQUALS

The current governor, Democrat Gray Davis, was elected in 1998 and reelected in 2002 (Table 7.1). With an annual salary of $175,000, he is the third highest-paid chief executive of the fifty states, trailing only New York and Michigan. As California's highest-ranking executive, the governor is the state's chief administrator, unofficial leader of his political party, and liaison to other states, the U.S. government, and other nations.

No stranger to California politics, current Governor Gray Davis was first elected to the assembly in 1982, followed by elections to state

TABLE 7.1
CALIFORNIA GOVERNORS AND THEIR PARTIES, 1943–2003

NAME	PARTY	DATES IN OFFICE
Earl Warren	Republican*	1943–1953
Goodwin J. Knight	Republican	1953–1959
Edmund G. Brown, Sr.	Democrat	1959–1967
Ronald Reagan	Republican	1967–1975
Jerry Brown	Democrat	1975–1983
George Deukmejian	Republican	1983–1991
Pete Wilson	Republican	1991–1999
Gray Davis	Democrat	1999–2007

*Warren cross-filed as both a Republican and a Democrat in 1946 and 1950.

controller (1986–1994) and lieutenant governor (1994–1998). Unlike his conservative Republican predecessor Pete Wilson, Davis emphasizes traditional Democratic Party issues. He has favored pouring state dollars into what he has described as a woefully underfinanced public education and public transportation systems, commitments that were scaled back when the state suffered a drastic budget crunch in 2002. At the same time, he has advocated gun control and sought middle ground on affirmative action. Davis is closely aligned with environmentalist, organized labor, gay and lesbian rights, and pro-choice elements of his party. Yet, he has also embraced traditional Republican components of capital punishment and tough law enforcement as key elements of his own political philosophy.

Much of the governor's authority comes from formal powers written into the state's constitution and its laws. In addition, certain informal powers derive from the prestige that the governor acquires with the electorate during his or her stay in office.

FORMAL POWERS

No other formal power is more important than the governor's budgetary responsibilities. According to the constitution, the governor must recommend a balanced budget to the legislature within the first ten days of each calendar year. The governor's proposals usually include requests for both taxing and spending. Budget work is virtually a year-round task for the governor and his or her appointed **director of finance.** The two begin their initial preparations on July 1, the start of the fiscal year, and end with the signing of the budget about a year later.

The state constitution requires the legislature to respond to the governor's budget no later than June 15 so that the budget can go into effect by July 1, a formidable task because the proposed document is the size of a thick telephone book. Technically, legislators can disregard any or all parts of the budget package and pass their own version, but usually they stay reasonably close to the governor's proposals.

The legislators' acquiescence in the budgetary process reflects their recognition of political realities more than their deference to the governor. They realize that the governor has the final say, albeit with some limitations. The governor cannot add money, but he or she can reduce or eliminate expenditures through use of the item veto before signing the budget into law. An absolute two-thirds vote from each house of the legislature, a near-impossibility (see Chapter 5), is necessary to overturn item vetoes. Accordingly, legislators often attempt to head off vetoes by negotiating with the governor in advance.

Whereas the **item veto** is restricted to appropriations measures, the **general veto** allows the governor to reject any other bill passed by the legislature. It, too, can be overturned only by an absolute two-thirds vote in each house. As with predecessors George Deukmejian and Pete Wilson, Gray Davis has exercised general and item vetoes without a single one being overturned by the legislature. Indeed, he has used the veto more than any governor in recent memory. During the 2000–2001 legislative year alone, Davis vetoed a record one-fourth of all bills passed by the legislature. Thus, the veto is a particularly important weapon in the governor's political arsenal (Table 7.2).

Under most circumstances, the governor has twelve days to act after the legislature passes a bill. On the hundreds of bills enacted by the legislature at session's end, however, the governor has thirty days to act. Only a veto can keep a bill from becoming law. After the governor's time limit has passed, any unsigned or unvetoed bill becomes law the following January (unless the bill is an urgency measure, in which case it takes effect immediately).

TABLE 7.2
VETOES AND OVERRIDES, 1967–2002

GOVERNOR	BILLS VETOED	VETOES OVERRIDDEN
Ronald Reagan (1967–1975)	7.3%	1
Jerry Brown (1975–1983)	6.3%	13
George Deukmejian (1983–1991)	15.1%	0
Pete Wilson (1991–1999)	16.6%	0
Gray Davis (1999-2002)	19.4%	0

If the governor believes that the legislature has not addressed an important issue, he or she can take the dramatic step of calling a special session. On such occasions, the lawmakers must discuss only the specific business proposed by the governor. Sometimes special sessions are called to meet unexpected crises, as in 2001, when Governor Gray Davis asked the legislature to deal with California's energy crisis. More often, the governor calls a special session simply to get the legislature to focus on a particularly thorny issue, such as in 1999, when Governor Davis asked the legislature to reform the state's public education system.

The governor's appointment powers, although substantial, are somewhat more restricted than his or her budgetary authority because all appointments except personal staff must be approved by others. Moreover, gubernatorial appointees hold only the top policymaking positions in the state system. Before the Progressive reforms, California governors could rely on patronage, or the "spoils" system, to hire friends or political allies. Today, 99 percent of all state employees are not appointed by the governor but rather are selected through a civil service system based on merit. The governor still fills about 2,500 key positions in the executive departments and cabinet agencies, except for the Departments of Justice and Education, whose heads are elected by the public. Together these appointees direct the state bureaucracy (Figure 7.1).

Most of the governor's appointees must be approved by the state senate. Generally, senate confirmation is routine, but occasionally the governor's choice for a key post is rejected for reasons other than qualifications. On the rare occasions when individuals elected to the executive branch vacate their posts, such as the opening created by the departure of Insurance Commissioner Chuck Quackenbush in 2000, the governor's nominees must be approved by majorities in both houses of the legislature.

The governor also appoints people to more than 100 state boards and commissions. Membership on some boards, such as the Arts Council and the Commission on Aging, which have only advisory authority, is largely ceremonial. Other boards, however, such as the California Energy Commission (CEC), the Public Utilities Commission (PUC), the California Coastal Commission (CCC), and the California Occupational Health and Safety Administration (Cal-OSHA), make important policies, free from gubernatorial control.

Nevertheless, the governor affects key "independent" boards through manipulation of the budget. One telling example occurred in 1993, when Republican Governor Wilson eliminated funding for the State Finance Commission, which, coincidentally, was chaired by then-State Treasurer and future opponent Kathleen Brown. The governor reasoned that the commission's functions duplicated those of other state units, but Treasurer Brown replied that Wilson was simply out to "silence a respected voice" of fiscal responsibility.[1]

FIGURE 7.1

STATE DEPARTMENTS AND AGENCIES

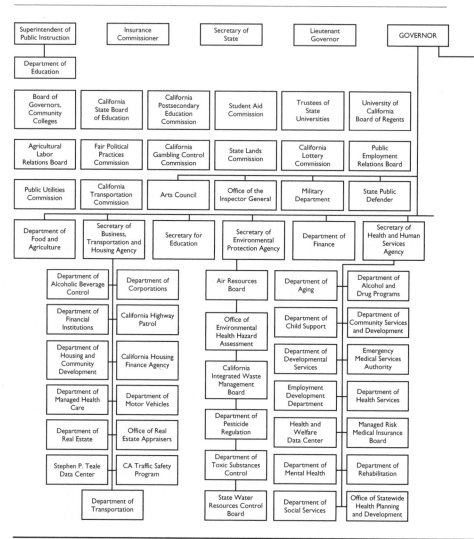

SOURCE: Office of the Governor.

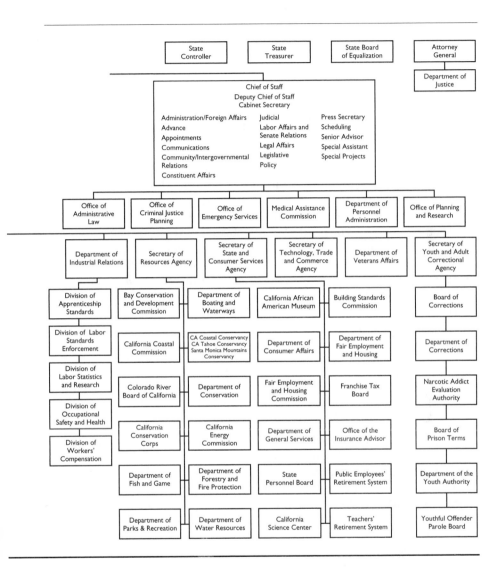

Perhaps the most enduring of all gubernatorial appointments are judgeships. The governor fills both vacancies and new judgeships that are periodically created by the legislature. In his eight years as governor, Pete Wilson filled 693 posts. During his first term, Gray Davis appointed 232 judges. Most judges continue to serve long after those who appointed them have gone. However, the governor's power is checked here, too, by various judicial commissions and by the voters in future elections (see Chapter 6).

INFORMAL POWERS

Formal constraints on the governor can be offset to some extent by a power that is not written into the constitution at all: the governor's popularity. As the top state official, the governor is highly visible. The attention focused on the office provides a platform from which he or she can influence the public and overcome political opponents.

California's governors historically have used the prestige of their office to push their own agendas. Among the recent occupants, George Deukmejian won public support with campaigns for capital punishment and against higher state taxes; he lost ground by opposing ballot propositions to restore the state's principal health and safety agency (OSHA), increase cigarette taxes, reduce insurance rates, and give more money to public education.

Throughout his tenure as governor, Pete Wilson engaged the legislature in protracted budget battles. During most of his eight years in office, he demanded massive cuts in welfare and virtually all other elements of state spending in return for levying no new taxes. Only prisons consistently received Wilson's blessing as recipients of new spending. Almost always the legislature capitulated after symbolic resistance. More than any governor in recent times, Wilson used ballot propositions for public policymaking. In 1994 he led the way on **Proposition 187,** an attempt to reduce government benefits to illegal immigrants that was ultimately declared unconstitutional by the federal courts. In 1996 Wilson championed **Proposition 209,** entitled the California Civil Rights Initiative, as a means of eliminating affirmative action. And in 1998 he promoted **Proposition 227,** an initiative on restricting bilingual education. Clearly, Wilson won more than his share of statewide ballot proposition victories.

Gray Davis has brought his unique brand of politics to the governor's office as well, thanks largely to unanticipated circumstances. When the state was suddenly confronted by a severe energy shortage in 2001, Davis acted on several fronts. Using his executive powers, he relaxed the state's air standards to permit older, dirtier electricity plants to produce more energy. At the same time, he signed an executive order that allowed the CEC to expedite the approval process for new power plants.

Meanwhile, he called upon the Federal Energy Regulatory Commission to establish price caps, a step taken by the agency nearly one year later. Davis blamed the state's sudden shortages on the energy producer "robber barons,"[2] and demanded the return of more than $9 billion in overcharges to California consumers. By 2002, documents provided by Enron Corporation, an abruptly bankrupt energy company, supported Davis's claim of corporate collusion.[3] Capturing any of the overcharges, however, remained a challenge. Between the energy crisis and huge budget shortfall of 2002 (see Chapter 8), Davis has been confronted with unprecedented challenges. There is little doubt that he has made his mark on the state, although raising eyebrows from some observers along the way. Thus, when discussing legislators in 1999, Davis stated that "their job is to implement my vision."[4] Davis offered similar advice to the state's judiciary in 2000 when he declared that "my [judicial] appointees should reflect my views. They are not here to be independent agents."[5] Such comments might seem harsh, especially to defenders of other branches of government, but they are vintage Davis nonetheless.

THE SUPPORTING CAST

If California's executive branch were composed solely of the governor, appointed department heads, and the civil service system, it would parallel the federal executive branch. However, the state's executive branch also includes a lieutenant governor, an attorney general, a secretary of state, a controller, a treasurer, an insurance commissioner, a superintendent of public instruction, and a five-member Board of Equalization. All are elected at the same time and serve four-year terms, but unlike the president and vice president, who are elected on the same political party ticket, each of these officeholders runs independently.

Most other states provide for the election of a lieutenant governor, a secretary of state, a treasurer, and an attorney general, but few elect an education officer, a controller, a Board of Equalization, and an insurance regulator. Moreover, most states call for the governor and the lieutenant governor (and others in some cases) to run as a team, thus providing some executive branch cohesion. Not so in California, where, as a result of independent contests, each elected member of the executive branch is beholden to no one.

The consequences of this system can be quite serious. For example, when Republican Governor Wilson ordered then-Controller Gray Davis, a Democrat, to cut state employee paychecks by 5 percent as part of the state's deficit-reduction package in 1991, Davis refused. Likewise, in 2002, when Governor Davis said that the state would not be able to send welfare checks before the passage of a stalled state budget, he was over-ruled by fellow Democrat State Controller Kathleen Connell, the individual who actually signed the checks. These examples show the extent to which very public fights may occur between two officeholders in the executive branch.

THE LIEUTENANT GOVERNOR

The **lieutenant governor** is basically an executive-in-waiting with few formal responsibilities. Should the governor become disabled or be out of state, the lieutenant governor fills in as acting governor. Should the governor leave office, the lieutenant governor takes over. This has happened seven times in the state's history, most recently in 1953, when Goodwin Knight stepped in after Governor Earl Warren became chief justice of the U.S. Supreme Court. The current lieutenant governor, Democrat Cruz Bustamante, was elected in 1998 and reelected in 2002. His election is significant for two reasons: First, as a Democrat, Bustamante ended a twenty-year pattern that witnessed the top two officeholders from different political parties. Second, he is the first Latino to hold statewide office in California since 1872.

The lieutenant governor heads some units, such as the State Lands Commission and the Commission on Economic Development. He or she also serves as president of the state senate, but this job, too, is long on title and short on substance. As senate president, the lieutenant governor may vote to break 20–20 ties, an event that last occurred in 1976. So minimal are the responsibilities of the lieutenant governor that one recent holder of the job quipped that his biggest daily task was to wake up, check the morning newspaper to see if the governor had died, and then return to bed![6] That description may stretch the point a bit, but not by much, according to many political observers.

THE ATTORNEY GENERAL

Despite the lieutenant governor's higher rank, the **attorney general** is usually considered the second-most powerful member of the executive branch. As head of the Department of Justice, the attorney general oversees law enforcement activities, acts as legal counsel to state agencies, represents the state in important cases, and renders opinions on (interprets) proposed and existing laws. The current attorney general, Democrat Bill Lockyer, was elected to the office for the first time in 1998 and reelected in 2002. He has used the powers of his office to enforce assault weapons legislation. But Lockyer has gained even greater notoriety through his high-profile suits against several energy companies for unjust profits and against Microsoft for antitrust violations.

Substantial authority and independent election allow the attorney general to chart a course separate from the governor's on important state questions. For example, in 1987 then-Attorney General John Van de Kamp, a Democrat, refused to represent Republican Governor Deukmejian in a lawsuit over Deukmejian's management of a new law, forcing the governor to hire private counsel at state expense. Such power gives the attorney general a high public profile, enhancing both the clout and the political standing of the officeholder. Earl Warren, Edmund G. "Pat" Brown, and George Deukmejian all moved up to the governor's office from the position of attorney general.

THE SECRETARY OF STATE

Unlike the U.S. cabinet official who bears the same title, the **secretary of state** of California is basically a records keeper and elections supervisor. The job entails certifying the number and validity of signatures obtained for initiatives, referenda, and recall petitions; producing sample ballots and ballot arguments for the voters; publishing official election results; and keeping the records of the legislature and the executive branch. During his tenure in the office, Republican Bill Jones upgraded the Web site of the Secretary of State's office, increasing accessibility to campaign and lobbying records.

The current secretary of state, Democrat Kevin Shelley, was elected in 2002. A former assembly member from San Francisco, Shelley co-authored Proposition 41 in 2002, a $200 million bond proposition that provided funds for counties to improve voting machines.

THE SUPERINTENDENT OF PUBLIC INSTRUCTION

The **superintendent of public instruction** heads the Department of Education. He or she is the only elected official in the executive branch chosen by nonpartisan ballot. Candidates are identified only by their names and vocations on the primary ballot. Unless one wins a majority, the top two face each other in the November general election. The current superintendent of public instruction, former Democratic state senator Jack O'Connell, was elected in 2002. While in the legislature, he authored Proposition 39 in 2000, which reduced the requirements for local school bonds passage from two-thirds to 55 percent.

In general, the electorate knows little about the candidates. But teachers' unions, education administrators, and other affected groups take great interest in the choice of superintendent because this official oversees California's massive public education system. The superintendent's powers are severely limited, however, because funding is determined largely by the governor's budgetary decisions, and policies are closely watched by the governor-appointed state board of education and the education committees of the legislature.

THE MONEY OFFICERS

Perhaps the most fractured part of the executive branch is the group of elected officials who manage the state's money. Courtesy of the Progressive reformers who feared a concentration of power, the controller, the treasurer, and the Board of Equalization have separate but overlapping responsibilities in this area. The **controller** supervises all state and local tax collection and writes checks for the state, including those to state employees. The controller is also an *ex officio* (automatically, by virtue of the office) member of several agencies, including the Board of Equalization, the Franchise Tax Board, and the State Lands Commission. Of all the "money officers," the controller is the most powerful and thus the most prominent. The current controller, Democrat and former high-tech executive Steve Westly, was elected in 2002 in his first try for statewide office.

Between taxing and spending, the **treasurer** invests state funds until they are needed for expenditures. Phil Angelides, former state Democratic party chair, was elected to this office in 1998 and reelected in 2002. For years, the treasurer's position remained almost hidden from public view because of inactivity. But with the growing importance of short-term investments, especially during lean budget years, the office has become better known. In 2002 Angelides used the powers of his office to refinance California's long-term debt, saving the state $1 billion.[7]

The **Board of Equalization** is also part of California's fiscal system. A product of reform efforts to ensure fair taxation, it oversees the collection of excise taxes on sales, gasoline, and liquor. The board also reviews county assessment practices to ensure uniform calculation methods and practices. The board has five members—four who are elected in districts of equal population and the controller, who serves as chair. Because its tasks lie in the backwaters of state politics, the board's incumbents usually return again and again. Many critics say that the board is an unnecessary vestige of the past; nevertheless, all efforts to eliminate it have proved unsuccessful.

THE INSURANCE COMMISSIONER

The office of **insurance commissioner** exemplifies the persistent reform mentality of California voters. Until 1988 the office was part of the state's Business, Housing, and Transportation Agency. But soaring insurance rates led to Proposition 103, a 1988 initiative that called for 20 percent across-the-board reductions in insurance premiums and made the position of insurance commissioner elective. The scandal surrounding the tenure of Insurance Commissioner Chuck Quackenbush (1994–2000) once again raised the question of whether this office should be elective.

The first elected insurance commissioner, Democrat John Garamendi (1990–1994), obtained about $700 million of the possible $2.5 billion in rebates resulting from Proposition 103. In 1994 Garamendi's successor, Republican Chuck Quackenbush, pursued a policy of insurance industry self-regulation rather than rebates. His approach drew considerable criticism after the massive 1994 Northridge earthquake. Public records showed that several insurance companies had intentionally mishandled claims, leading department staff to recommend hundreds of millions of dollars in fines. Instead, Quackenbush allowed token contributions to his favorite charities and foundations as payment.[8] This arrangement provoked an investigation by the legislature, which led to Quackenbush's resignation in July 2000. Retired state appeals court Judge Henry Low, nominated by Governor Davis to complete Quackenbush's term, chose not to run in 2002.

John Garamendi was once again elected insurance commissioner in 2002. Attempting to show independence, Garamendi campaigned for the post without taking any money from insurance interests.

THE BUREAUCRACY

Elected officials are just the most observable part of the state's administrative machinery. Backing them up, implementing their programs, and dealing with citizens on a daily basis are more than 275,000 state workers–the bureaucracy. Only about 5,000 of these workers are appointed by the governor or by other executive officers. Of the rest, 90,000 work at the University of California and California State University. The remainder are hired and fired through the state civil service system on the basis of their examination results, performance, and job qualifications. The Progressives designed this system to insulate government workers from political influences and to make them more professional than those who might be hired out of friendship.

The task of the bureaucracy is to carry out the programs established by the policymaking institutions–the executive branch, the legislature, and the judiciary, along with a handful of regulatory agencies. However, because bureaucrats are permanent, full-time professionals, they sometimes influence the content of programs and policies, chiefly by advising public officials or by exercising the discretion built into the laws that define bureaucratic tasks. The bureaucracy may also influence policy through the lobbying efforts of its employee organizations (see Chapter 4).

State bureaucrats work for various departments and agencies (Figure 7.1), each run by an administrator appointed by the governor and confirmed by the senate. Although civil servants are permanent employees, most administrators serve at the governor's pleasure and must resign upon his or her demand. Sometimes political appointees and civil servants clash over the best ways to carry out state policy. Should the bureaucracy become too independent, the governor can always use his or her budgetary powers to bring it back into line.

MAKING THE PIECES FIT

The executive branch is a hodgepodge of separately elected authorities who serve in overlapping and conflicting institutional positions. Nobody, not even the governor, is really in charge. Each official simply attempts to carry out his or her mission with the hope that passable policy will result. Occasionally, reformers have suggested streamlining the system by consolidating functions and reducing the number of elective offices, but the only recent change has been the addition of yet another office, that of insurance commissioner. In 2002, Democrats reached a milestone when they won every statewide office for the first time since 1882.

Despite these obstacles, officeholders—most notably governors—have been able to effect some change. George Deukmejian appointed conservative judges, toughened law enforcement, promoted new prisons, and loosened a multitude of regulations on business. Pete Wilson waged war against illegal immigrants, affirmative action, and bloated welfare while continuing to trumpet the "law-and-order" theme. Gray Davis was instrumental in responding to the state's power shortage crisis.

But the governor does not operate alone. He or she must contend with other executive branch members, a suspicious legislature, independent courts, a professional bureaucracy, and most of all, an electorate with a highly erratic collective pulse. Whether these conditions are challenges or impediments, they make the executive branch an interesting part of California government.

Notes

1. "Wilson Cuts Funding for State Finance Commission," *Los Angeles Times,* July 2, 1993, p. A1.
2. "Davis Takes on 'Robber Barons'," *San Francisco Chronicle,* June 17, 2001, p. A16.
3. "Californians Call Enron Documents The Smoking Gun," *The New York Times,* May 8, 2002, pp. 1A, C6.

4. "Tensions Flare Between Davis and His Democrats," *Los Angeles Times,* July 22, 1999, pp. A1, A28.

5. "Davis Comments Draw Fire," *San Jose Mercury News,* March 1, 2000, p. 14A.

6. "The Most Invisible Job in Sacramento," *Los Angeles Times,* May 10, 1998, pp. A1, A20.

7. "Angelides: Refinance to Trim Deficit," *Los Angeles Times,* January 4, 2002, pp. B1, B10.

8. See "Quackenbush Rejected Steep Fines for Insurers," *Los Angeles Times,* April 2, 2000, pp. A1, A26.

Learn More on the World Wide Web

Office of the Attorney General: www.caag.state.ca.us

Office of the Governor: www.ca.gov

Office of the Lieutenant Governor: www.ltg.ca.gov

Office of the Secretary of State: www.ss.ca.gov

Office of the State Board of Equalization: www.boe.ca.gov

Office of the State Controller: www.sco.ca.gov

Office of the State Insurance Commissioner: www.insurance.ca.gov

Office of the State Treasurer: www.treasurer.ca.gov

Office of the Superintendent of Public Instruction: www.cde.ca.gov/executive

Learn More at the Library

Gary G. Hamilton and Nicole Woolsey Biggart, *Governor Reagan, Governor Brown: A Sociology of Executive Power,* New York: Columbia University Press, 1984.

Gerald C. Lubenow, ed., *California Votes: The 1998 Governor's Race,* Berkeley: Institute of Governmental Studies, University of California, 1999.

CHAPTER 8

TAXING AND SPENDING: BUDGETARY POLITICS AND POLICIES

■══════■

No issue is more critical to Californians than taxation. And no resource is more important to state policymakers than the revenues generated from taxation. Yet even though the public and elected officials may agree on the need for taxes, they often disagree on how much should be collected and where it should be spent. When policymakers seem to stray from public values with regard to budgetary issues, the voters are not shy about using the tools of direct democracy to reorder the state's fiscal priorities–and with the annual state budget at about $100 billion, much is at stake.

Unlike the national government, which usually operates with a deficit, states can spend only as much money as they collect. This has been difficult in California, where a steady flow of immigrants, a burgeoning school-age population, massive attention to crime, and reduced federal defense spending have tested a state budget process known more for its limits than for its vision. California fell on particularly hard times in 2002. After several years of revenue surpluses, the state suffered from recession. As a result, projected revenues and expenditures were out of balance by a whopping $24 billion, not only the largest in state history but more than the deficits of the other forty-nine states combined. Democratic Governor Gray Davis and Republican state legislators sparred over whether to raise taxes, cut services, or choose a combination. Predictably, they settled on the latter approach, but only after very ugly and public fights.

THE BUDGETARY PROCESS

Budget making is a complicated and lengthy activity in California. Participants include the governor and various executive branch departments, the legislature and its support agencies, the public (via the initiative and the referendum), and occasionally the courts when judges uphold or overturn commitments made by the other policymakers.

THE GOVERNOR AND OTHER EXECUTIVE OFFICERS

Preparation of the annual budget is the governor's most important formal power. Other policymakers participate in the budgetary process, but none has as much clout because the governor both frames the document before it goes to the legislature and refines the budget after it leaves the legislature through use of the item veto on budget items that he or she opposes.

During the preceding summer and fall, the governor's director of finance works closely with the budget heads of each state department. Supported by a staff of fiscal experts, the director of finance gathers and assesses information about the anticipated needs of each department and submits a "first draft" budget to the governor in the late fall. The governor presents a refined version of this draft to the legislature the following January. The state constitution gives the legislature until June 15 to respond. The annual budget is supposed to take effect on July 1, although it has been late for fourteen of the past twenty-five years. The 2002–2003 budget was not passed until August 31, making it the longest overdue budget since the legislature began meeting full-time in 1968.

LEGISLATIVE PARTICIPANTS

Legislative agreement on the budget is often difficult to achieve because, as a "money" bill, it requires an absolute two-thirds vote of approval in each house. Often completed well after the deadline, the budget is a blueprint for the state's annual policy commitments. But in a sense the final vote is anticlimactic because many crucial decisions are made earlier in the year.

Upon receiving the budget in January, the legislature's leaders do little more than refer the document to the legislative analyst. Over the next two months, the legislative analyst (currently Elizabeth Hill) and staff scrutinize each part of the budget with respect to needs, costs, and other factors. Often the analyst's findings clash with those of the governor, providing the legislature with an independent source of data and evaluation.

Meanwhile, two key legislative units—the Assembly Ways and Means Committee and the Senate Budget and Fiscal Review Committee—guide the budget proposal through the legislative process. After the committee staffs spend about two months going through the entire document, each house assigns portions to various committees and their staffs. During this time, lobbyists, individual citizens, government officials, and other legislators testify on the proposed budget before committees and subcommittees.

By mid-April the committees conclude their hearings, combine their portions into a single document, and bring the budget bill to their respective full houses for a vote. Should the houses differ on specifics, the bill goes to a two-house conference committee for reconciliation, after which both houses vote again. As June nears and the two houses hone their versions, key legislative leaders and the governor enter into informal negotiations over the document that the legislature and governor will ultimately approve. Known as the **Big Five,** this group becomes the nucleus of the final budgetary debate.

THE PUBLIC

Historically, the public has used initiatives or referenda to shape the budget. The voters have relied on ballot propositions to approve the sales tax (1933) and repeal the inheritance tax (1982). Perhaps the most dramatic tax-altering event came in 1978 with the passage of **Proposition 13,** an initiative that reduced local property taxes by 57 percent. Since 1978, property owners have saved more than $195 billion in taxes[1] while local governments have become increasingly dependent on the state for relief. As a result, the state has become the major funding agent for local services such as public education.

Voters dropped the other shoe on budget planning in 1979 with the passage of **Proposition 4,** a measure designed to limit state expenditure increases according to a precise formula based on the national Consumer Price Index (CPI) and on state population growth. In 1990 voters approved **Proposition 111,** a referendum that modified the Proposition 4 formula by replacing the national CPI with the state CPI in recognition of the high cost of living in California.

The voters addressed the tax issue again in 1993. After Governor Wilson redirected $2.4 billion in state funds from local governments to reduce the state's deficit, he and the legislature received voter approval of **Proposition 172,** a measure to increase the state sales tax by 0.5 percent. Passed in 1993, the proposition earmarked new revenues exclusively for local government public safety–related activities. In the same year, the voters passed **Proposition 218,** a measure requiring voter approval of all local government tax increases on property.

THE COURTS

Questions about the legality of various state taxes and programs sometimes make the courts major players in the budgetary process. Judicial involvement is necessary occasionally because of "quick fixes" to complex budget issues that are enacted by the public policy makers or the voters.

In 1994 state courts rejected Governor Wilson's plan to pay state workers with IOUs (officially known as "scrip") while he and the legislature fought over a deficit-riddled state budget. State Controller

Kathleen Connell suffered a similar fate in 1998 when a superior court judge blocked her from paying state workers and an array of state bills without a state budget in place. Even the will of the voters has been subject to judicial review, particularly in the many cases arising from the tax-limitation rules and procedures of Proposition 13.

REVENUE SOURCES

Like most states, California relies on several forms of taxation to fund its budget. The largest sources of revenue are the personal income tax, sales tax, and bank and corporation taxes. Smaller revenue supplies come from motor vehicle fuel, insurance, tobacco, and alcohol taxes. The state's major revenue sources and expenditures for fiscal year 2002–2003 are shown in Figure 8.1.

FIGURE 8.1
CALIFORNIA'S REVENUE SOURCES AND EXPENDITURES, 2002–2003

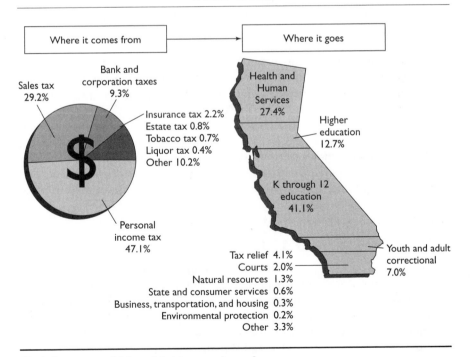

*Excludes motor vehicle–related taxes and user fees.

SOURCE: Governor's Office.

Other taxes are levied by local governments. Chief among these is the property tax, although its use was reduced considerably by Proposition 13. This tax is not collected by the state, but it still is a part, directly or indirectly, of the tax burden of all Californians.

All too aware of the state's antitax mood, policymakers have refused to add taxes to cope with burgeoning needs. As a result, the state's commitments to most services have decreased considerably in recent years. Individual recipients, school districts, and local governments have been thrown into turmoil; infrastructure work such as repairs after the 1989 and 1994 earthquakes and highway maintenance programs have been stretched out.

THE SALES TAX

Until the Great Depression of 1929, the relatively small state government relied on minor taxes on businesses and utilities for funds. After the economic crash, however, the state was forced to develop new tax sources to cope with hard times. The first of these, a 2.5 percent **sales tax,** was adopted to provide permanent funding for schools and local governments. Today the statewide sales tax is 7.25 percent; as much as 1.25 percent is tacked on by counties engaged in state-approved projects, most of which are transportation related. Of the basic 7.25 percent, cities and counties get 1.5 percent, county transit programs get 0.25 percent, and the state keeps the rest.

Occasionally, the legislature temporarily adjusts the sales tax upward or downward in response to economic conditions. Such an adjustment last occurred in December 1989, when, in response to the major earthquake in Northern California, the legislature and governor tacked on an additional 0.25 percent for thirteen months to pay for major road repairs. In 1991 Republican Governor Pete Wilson and the legislature agreed to cut sales taxes by 0.25 percent when the state enjoyed a budget surplus of 4 percent or more for two successive years. This reduction remained in place until 2002, when the revenue shortfall forced an adjustment upward. Today, the sales tax accounts for about 29 percent of the state's tax revenues.

THE PERSONAL INCOME TAX

A second major revenue source, the **personal income tax,** was modeled after its federal counterpart to collect greater amounts of money from those residents with greater earnings. Today the personal income tax varies between 1 and 9.3 percent, depending on one's income. State lawmakers and Governor Wilson increased the tax on the highest incomes to 11 percent in 1991, but Wilson argued for and won reduction to 9.3 percent beginning in January 1996.

The personal income tax is now the fastest-growing component of state revenue (Figure 8.2), a significant fact because Californians ranked eighth in per capita income in 2001. Inasmuch as the tax goes up with increasing incomes, it filled the state coffers with the dramatic economic recovery through most of the 1990s. As of 2002 the tax accounted for 47 percent of the state tax bite, down from 56 percent in 2000.

BANK AND CORPORATION TAXES

Financial industry and corporation taxes contribute much less than sales and personal income taxes. Taxes on banks and corporations did not exceed 5.5 percent until 1959, when the legislature enacted a series of upward rate changes. The last increase occurred in 1980, when,

FIGURE 8.2
CALIFORNIA'S TAX BURDEN, 1942–2002

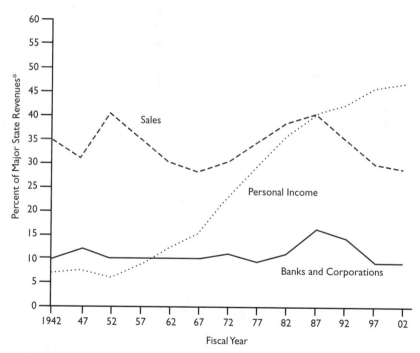

*Excludes motor vehicle-related taxes and user fees.

SOURCE: Governor's Office.

responding to local governments' losses from Proposition 13, the legislature boosted the **bank and corporation tax** from 9.6 percent to 11.6 percent. Between 1987 and 1996, however, the legislature reduced the tax to 8.8 percent, where it remains for corporations today. Since 1996 the corporate tax for banks has been fixed at 10.8 percent. Together, bank and corporation taxes now account for about 9 percent of state revenues.

Aside from Proposition 13 and the expanded reliance on **user taxes** such as those levied on gasoline and cigarettes, California's revenue collection system has undergone gradual adjustments over the past sixty years. Charted in Figure 8.2 are the changing influences of the sales, personal income, and bank and corporation taxes from 1942 to the present. Recent data indicate a steady drift toward increased dependence on the personal income tax and decreased dependence on sales taxes.

OTHER SOURCES

From time to time, state leaders have asked voters to approve bonds, thus obligating the electorate to long-term commitments. These projects, sometimes lasting as long as forty years, finance major infrastructure commitments such as school classrooms, highways, and water projects. The state has turned to bonds with increasing reliance. In 1991 California ranked thirty-second among the fifty states in indebtedness on a per capita basis; by 2001 the state had climbed to nineteenth place, with indebtedness of about $29 billion. The state's per capita indebtedness of $608 is now about 10 percent beyond the national average.

California also gets a small but growing portion of its revenue from fees and charges for services. For example, 90 percent of the operating costs of state parks were funded by taxes in 1982–1983, but within a decade, only 40 percent came from tax revenues, whereas 57 percent came from fees and concessions. Agreement by Governor Davis and the legislature to halve fees to most state parks in 2000 reversed the direction of some charges. Nevertheless, user fees accounted for 21 percent of all state revenues in 2000, compared with 18 percent at the beginning of the decade.

TAXES IN PERSPECTIVE

Viewed in comparison with other states, the overall tax burden for California ranks twelfth on a per capita basis. Recent figures show that the state has moved considerably from the "middle of the pack" status it had a decade earlier. That's because during the 1990s the state's economy grew 50 percent faster than the national average. Furthermore, although there have been changes in the state tax blend, California's position among the other states remains almost exactly where it was thirty years ago.

When calculating state and local taxes as a percentage of personal income, California ranks fifteenth. On a per capita basis, the state ranks seventeenth in sales taxes, ninth in personal income taxes, ninth in bank and corporation taxes, and thirty-third in property taxes. In other areas, California taxes are near the bottom. For example, the state ranks forty-ninth in fuel taxes and forty-ninth in alcoholic beverage taxes. Cigarette taxes stand out as a prominent exception due to a voter-approved initiative in 1998, which moved the state into third place behind Minnesota and Hawaii. Otherwise, powerful interest group lobbying has led California to rely less on "sin" taxes than do most other states, where liquor and gambling are lucrative sources of revenue.

Balancing budget revenues and expenditures has not always been easy for state leaders. Between 1991 and 1995 the state budgetary process was hobbled by an unrelenting recession and its by-product, inadequate revenues. Between 1991 and 1995 the state suffered annual budget shortfalls of anywhere between $5 billion and $14 billion, often forcing Governor Wilson and the recession-weary legislature to raise taxes and borrow billions from banks just to make ends meet. Beginning in 1996, the state recovered, leading to the huge surpluses of 1999 through 2001. As a result, Governor Davis and the legislature agreed on increased spending and a modest tax refund. The state economy soured considerably in 2002, leaving a huge revenue gap. Such ups and downs make it difficult for a state to plan long-term expenditures for infrastructure areas such as education, transportation, and resource management in any meaningful way; nevertheless, these undulations have become commonplace in the budget planning process.

SPENDING

The annual state budget addresses thousands of financial commitments, both large and small. Major areas of expenditure include public education (grades K through 12), health and welfare, higher education, and prisons. Outlays in these four areas account for more than 80 percent of the general fund. The remainder of the budget (the difference between total expenditures and the general fund) goes to designated long-term projects such as transportation, parks, and veterans' programs, many of which have been authorized by public ballot.

Since 1979 state spending has been determined more by the public than by the legislature and the governor. Under Proposition 4 (1979) and Proposition 111 (1990), budgets have been determined largely by formulas rather than by need. Despite new commitments to criminal incarceration and disproportionate increases in the numbers of K–12 students and welfare recipients, the state has used this method. Critics have characterized the formula approach as a political "straitjacket," unresponsive to changing times and needs, particularly in light of decreasing federal support and a shrinking defense industry in

California. Defenders of "formula government" argue that it is the only way to keep state leaders from operating with a "blank check."

PUBLIC EDUCATION: GRADES K THROUGH 12

With the state constitution giving public education a "superior right" to state funds, public schools get the largest share of state expenditures. Public education funding became largely a state government obligation in 1972, when, in **Serrano v. Priest,** the state supreme court held that local property tax–financed education violated "equal protection under the law" guarantees because of the per capita amounts that varied widely from district to district. With this decision, the state became the major funding source of public education.

State funding for public education has an uneven history. Between 1975 and the late 1980s, the state consistently reduced its per capita support for K–12 public education, shrinking it to 37 percent of the general fund in 1988. Amid growing concerns about weak funding and poor classroom performance, education reformers secured voter approval of **Proposition 98** in 1988, a measure that established 40 percent as a minimum funding threshold except in times of fiscal emergency. With new funds available, the state has poured money into reducing classroom sizes in grades K–3 and lengthened the school year from 180 to 190 days. In the 2000–2001 fiscal year, schools were allocated $32.5 billion, about 41 percent of the state revenues collected through taxation, the basis of the general fund. Still, at $6,800 per student, California expenditures remain more than $1,000 below the national average.

Even with recent infusions, however, per capita spending has slipped to thirty-eighth–this despite having one of the highest per capita incomes in the nation (Figure 8.3). California continues near bottom (forty-ninth) among the states in its student/teacher ratio (a commonly used criterion for assessing education effectiveness) and in reading achievement, and California ranks fiftieth in computers per classroom.[2] And the state's graduation rate has ranked thirty-seventh for more than a decade.

Renewed focus on education has brought about improvements in some areas. Although state students were near last place in math and reading scores as recently as 1998, they showed modest gains in 1999 and 2000. Yet striking disparities in education scores have continued between those who are fluent in English and those who are not.[3] With Latino and Asian American students accounting for 40 percent and 11 percent of the school populations, respectively, issues stemming from the language barrier can be formidable and long lasting. Passage of **Proposition 227** in 1998, a measure limiting bilingual education for non-English speaking students to one year, has added to the debate over how to "mainstream" the diverse California student community.

Nevertheless, the debate goes on. Some reformers are looking closely at "charter schools," community-controlled educational centers, as

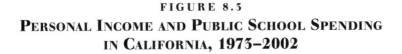

FIGURE 8.3

PERSONAL INCOME AND PUBLIC SCHOOL SPENDING IN CALIFORNIA, 1973–2002

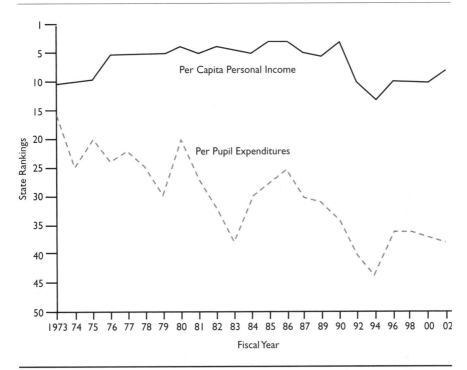

From Terry Christensen and Larry N. Gerston, *Politics in the Golden State: The California Connection*, 2nd ed., Glenview, IL: Scott, Foresman, 1988, p. 203; and California State Department of Education.

alternatives to what many describe as a broken system. Others have promoted vouchers, that is, cash payments for parents to select an education institution; the voters rejected such a measure in 2000, as they did in 1993. A recent U.S. Supreme Court decision allowing voucher programs may well lead to renewed consideration of the topic in California.[4]

PUBLIC EDUCATION: COLLEGES AND UNIVERSITIES

Three components share responsibility for higher education in California. The state's 108 two-year community colleges enroll about 1.5 million students. Funding for these institutions is connected to the primary and secondary public schools formula; to that extent, they have benefited from Proposition 98.

California also has two groups of four-year public institutions. With 188,000 students, the University of California (U.C.) educates both undergraduate and graduate students at 10 campuses throughout the state. Designated the state's primary research university, U.C. is the only public institution permitted to award professional degrees (such as medicine and law) and doctorates. The California State University system, with 389,000 students at 23 campuses, concentrates on undergraduate instruction, awarding master's degrees most commonly in such fields as education, engineering, and business.

State support for higher education was fairly consistent until the 1990s, holding at about 11 percent of the general-fund budget. Since the 1998–1999 fiscal year, the percentage of funding has increased, although it leveled off in 2002–2003, when the state provided $10 billion for higher education, or 12.7 percent of the general fund.

HEALTH AND HUMAN SERVICES

Health and human services programs receive the second-largest share of the state budget. Those programs accounting for the most significant state commitment include Aid to Families with Dependent Children (AFDC), Medi-Cal, and the Supplemental Security Income (SSI) program. Medi-Cal provides health care benefits for the poor; SSI offers state assistance to the elderly and the disabled. But no program carries the political charge of AFDC, which is the primary component of the state's welfare budget.

California has sizable welfare costs. With about 12 percent of the nation's population, the state has 16 percent of all welfare recipients. Only a decade ago California had 10.5 percent of the population and 12 percent of all welfare recipients.

Throughout his tenure as governor, Pete Wilson asserted that California's welfare payments were too high, particularly given the state's budget crunch. Most legislators found it politically difficult to oppose him. Between 1991 and 1999, average monthly state payments for three-member families in the AFDC program dropped from $693 to $609. With new federal legislation, the state's major welfare program changed to the Temporary Assistance for Needy Families Program (TANF) in 1997, which limited welfare payments to no more than five years. As of 2002–2003, health and human service programs accounted for about 27.4 percent of the general fund. Average welfare payments were $644 per month in 2000, still well below the figure from a decade ago.

PRISONS

Among the major recipients of state allocations, prison and corrections budgets have grown the most in recent years. As with education, the public has played a role in this policy area. In 1982 voters passed

Proposition 8, commonly known as The Victims' Bill of Rights, an initiative that established mandatory prison terms for various crimes and extended the terms for many other crimes. Even more sweeping changes occurred in 1994, when the legislature, and later the voters, enacted a new "get tough" law commonly referred to as the "three strikes" law (as in "three strikes and you're out"). This new law required a sentence of twenty-five years to life for anyone convicted of three felonies.

As a result of these policy changes, California's prison population has swelled beyond belief. Between 1976 and 1982 the state prison population grew by 60 percent, from 20,000 to 32,000. After the passage of Proposition 8, the prison population jumped to 162,136 in 1999, a staggering 407 percent increase. And as of 1999 prisons were operating at nearly 200 percent of capacity. Remarkably, the 45,527 corrections employees in 1998 actually exceeded the entire number of inmates incarcerated in 1982. But in 2000, the state prison population declined by 360 inmates, the first dip since 1977, leading some observers to wonder whether the state's "get tough" laws and expanding economy had finally turned the tide. About 7 percent of the state's general fund was used for youth and adult corrections during the 2002–2003 fiscal year.

MODERN STATE BUDGETS: TOO LITTLE, TOO MUCH, OR JUST RIGHT?

Have you ever met anyone who claims that he or she should pay more taxes? Neither have we. Almost everybody dislikes paying taxes, and almost everybody thinks the money collected is spent incorrectly. However, although most people oppose increased taxes, they also oppose program cuts. In fact, as the state surplus swelled in 2000, 67 percent of the respondents in a statewide survey said that they would prefer using the surplus for state and local services such as education, law enforcement, and transportation, compared with 20 percent who called for a rebate.[5] Now the surplus is gone, and in the wake of the September 11, 2001, terrorist attacks on the United States, the state must find hundreds of millions—perhaps billions—of dollars to pay for its share of homeland security, adding more pressure to the budget debate.[6]

Like their counterparts elsewhere, California policymakers have struggled to find a fair system of taxation to pay for needed programs. Given the involvement of so many public and private interests, however, fairness is difficult to determine. Moreover, during the past few decades, taxation and budget decisions have been subject to radical change. Somehow the state's infrastructure has survived, although critics have been less than thrilled with the fiscal uncertainty that has become commonplace in California government.

Notes

1. Howard Jarvis Taxpayers Association, www.hjta.org/about1.htm.
2. "Governor Signs Budget with Major K-14 Boost," press release, California Teachers Association, July 6, 2000.
3. "Stanford 9 Scores Paint a Picture of Contrasts in State," *Los Angeles Times,* July 23, 1999, pp. A1, A24.
4. In the 2002 case, *Zelman v. Simmons-Harris* (00-1751), the U.S. Supreme Court endorsed a Cleveland voucher program, leading one California expert to suggest that "it's going to add legitimacy to vouchers." See "Supreme Court, 5-4, Upholds Voucher System That Pays Religious Schools' Tuition," *The New York Times,* June 26, 2002, pp. A1, A17.
5. "More voters are in a spending than a tax rebating mood when it comes to the state surplus," The Field Poll, Release 1952, February 14, 2000, p. 3.
6. According to California Highway Patrol Commissioner D. O. "Spike" Helmick, the costs for additional law enforcement alone are expected to be near $2 billion. See "Mounting Costs Worry Safety Agencies," *Sacramento Bee,* November 16, 2001, p. 1A.

Learn More on the World Wide Web

California Budget Project: www.cbp.org

California State budget: www.dof.ca.gov; www.lao.ca.gov

California Taxpayers Association: www.caltax.org

National Governors' Association: www.nga.org

Learn More at the Library

David C. Nice, *Policy Innovation in State Government,* Ames: Iowa State University Press, 1994.

George R. Zodrow, *State Sales and Income Taxes: An Economic Analysis,* College Station: Texas A&M University Press, 1999.

CHAPTER 9

LOCAL GOVERNMENT: POLITICS AT THE GRASSROOTS

Both citizens and the media tend to focus on state and national politics, but local government activities often have a greater impact on our daily lives. Cities, counties, and school districts make decisions affecting the traffic on our streets, the quality (and quantity) of our water, the comfort and safety of our neighborhoods, the education of our children, and the assistance available to those of us who fall on hard times. Local government is also where citizens can have their greatest influence, simply because it is closer than Sacramento or Washington, D.C.

Although local governments are accountable to the citizens they serve, they are also agencies of the state. Local governments are created by state law, which assigns them their rights and duties, mandating some functions and activities and prohibiting others. The state also allocates taxing powers and shares revenues with local government. But the state can change the rights and powers granted to local governments at any time, expanding or reducing their tasks, their funding, and their independence.

COUNTIES AND CITIES

California's 58 counties and 476 cities were created in slightly different ways and perform distinctly different tasks.

COUNTIES

California is divided into **counties** (see the map on the inside front cover), ranging in size from San Francisco's 49 square miles to San Bernardino County's 20,164 and in population from Alpine County's 1,208 residents to Los Angeles County's 9,519,338. Counties function both as local governments and as administrative units of the state. As local governments, counties run jails, provide police and fire protection, maintain roads, and perform other services for rural and unincorporated areas (those that are not part of any city). They also operate transit systems, protect health and sanitation, and keep records on property, marriages, and deaths. As agencies of the state, counties oversee elections, operate the courts, administer the state's welfare system, and collect some state taxes.

The state's **general law** on counties prescribes the organization of county government. A county's central governing body is a five-member **board of supervisors,** whom voters elect by districts to staggered four-year terms. The board sets county policies and oversees the budget, usually hiring a chief administrator or **county executive** to carry out its programs. Besides the members of the board of supervisors, the voters elect the sheriff, the district attorney, the tax assessor, and other departmental executives (Figure 9.1). Conflicts often occur as the elected board tries to manage the budget and the elected executives attempt to deliver services. Unlike most of their state counterparts, these local officials are chosen in nonpartisan elections, a Progressive legacy that keeps party labels off the ballot; all serve four-year terms.

FIGURE 9.1

COUNTY GOVERNMENT: AN ORGANIZATIONAL CHART FOR CALIFORNIA'S FORTY-FIVE GENERAL-LAW COUNTIES

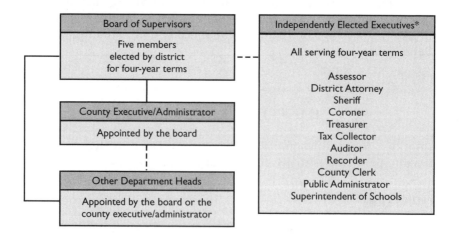

* Charter counties usually elect only the sheriff, assessor, and district attorney

Although most counties operate under this general-law system, twelve have exercised a state-provided option to organize their own governmental structures through documents called **charters.** Most of these charter counties, including Los Angeles, Sacramento, San Diego, and Santa Clara, are highly urbanized. County voters must approve the charter and any proposed amendments. Generally, "home rule" or charter counties use their local option to replace elected county administrators with appointees of the board of supervisors or to strengthen the powers of the county administrator. Voters in Los Angeles County recently used their charter authority to increase the size of their board of supervisors from five to nine, to provide better representation.

San Francisco is unique in California local government, functioning both as a city and as a county. Most counties have several cities within their boundaries, but the separate city and county governments of San Francisco were consolidated in 1911. San Francisco thus has a board of supervisors with eleven members rather than a city council, but unlike any other county, it has a mayor.

No new county has been formed in California since 1907, although in some large counties, such as Los Angeles, San Bernardino, and Santa Barbara, rural areas frustrated by urban domination have tried unsuccessfully to break away and form their own jurisdictions. The proponents of "Canyon County," in the northwest portion of Los Angeles County, have been particularly persistent in their efforts.

CITIES

Whereas counties are created by the state, **cities** are established at the request of their citizens, through the process of **incorporation.** As an unincorporated area urbanizes, residents begin to demand more services than the county can deliver. These may include police and fire protection, street maintenance, water, or other services. (Sewage treatment, for example, was the primary issue in the 1990 incorporation of Malibu, an affluent suburb of Los Angeles.) Residents may also wish to form a city to preserve the identity of their community or to avoid being annexed by some other city. Wealthy areas sometimes incorporate to protect their tax resources or their ethnic homogeneity from the impact of an adjacent big city and its economic and racial problems.

Whatever the motivation, the process of incorporation starts with a petition from the community's citizens. Then the county's **local agency formation commission** (LAFCO) determines whether the new city makes social and economic sense. If LAFCO approves, the county board of supervisors holds a hearing and then the voters approve or reject the incorporation.

Once formed, cities expand by annexing unincorporated (county) territory. Sometimes small cities that can't provide adequate services disband themselves by consolidating with an adjacent city. More rarely, residents of an existing city seek to deannex or secede. Such is currently the case with some parts of Los Angeles. The 222-square-mile San Fernando Valley hosts one-third of the population of Los Angeles, but many residents feel isolated and ignored by their city government. The Los Angeles County LAFCO approved their petition to secede, which placed the proposal on the ballot in November 2002, along with a similar proposal for secession by Hollywood. Secession required approval by the voters of both these areas and the city as a whole, however, and the voters of Los Angeles rejected the plan. But unless the discontent of the San Fernando Valley and other parts of Los Angeles is resolved, agitation for secession is likely to continue.

Like California counties, most California cities operate under the state's general law, which prescribes their governmental structure. General-law cities typically have a five-member **city council,** with members elected in nonpartisan elections for four-year terms. The council appoints a **city manager** to supervise daily operations; the manager, in turn, appoints department heads such as the police and fire chiefs (Figure 9.2).

Cities with populations exceeding 3,500 may exercise the option to write their own charters. A hundred and one California cities have done so. A charter city has more discretion in choosing the structure of its government than does a general-law city. It also has more freedom to

---

FIGURE 9.2

City Government: An Organizational Chart for California's General-Law Cities

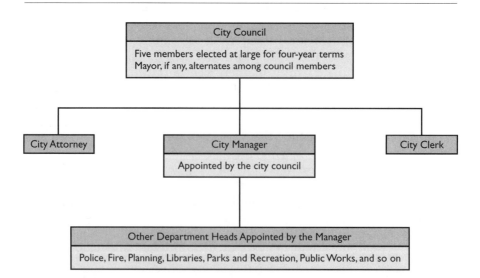

levy taxes not specifically forbidden by state law and to set policies that no state law supersedes. Most of the state's larger cities have their own charters to achieve greater flexibility in dealing with their complex problems.

Whether operating under general law or a home rule charter, once incorporated, a city takes on extensive responsibilities for local services, including police and fire protection, sewage treatment, garbage disposal, parks and recreational services, streets and traffic management, library operation, and land use planning. The county, however, still provides courts, jails, welfare, elections, tax collection, public health, and public transit.

POWER IN THE CITY: COUNCIL MEMBERS, MANAGERS, AND MAYORS

Almost all of California's cities have five-member city councils with appointed city managers as executives, as set forth in the state's general law. Some cities, particularly older and larger communities, have developed municipal government structures uniquely suited to their own needs and preferences. City councils, for example, may be chosen in a variety of ways or expanded in size to allow for more representation. Los Angeles has fifteen council members, San Jose ten, and San Diego eight. San Francisco's board of supervisors has eleven members. The executive office also varies among these cities; some opt for a stronger mayor rather than the manager prescribed by general law. When cities choose among these structures, they are allocating power in their communities.

ELECTIONS

In most California cities, each council member is chosen by the whole city in **at-large elections.** This system was created by the Progressives to replace **district elections,** in which each council member represented only part of the city. At-large elections were intended to reduce the parochial influence of machine-organized ethnic neighborhoods on the city as a whole. The strategy worked, but as a result, ethnic minority candidates, unable to secure enough votes from other areas of the city to win at large, were rarely elected. As cities grew, citywide campaigns also became extremely costly. The Progressives added to the difficulties of minority candidates and further raised the costs of campaigns by making local elections nonpartisan. This weakened the old party machines, but voters lost the modest cue provided by the listing of parties on the ballot, minority candidates were denied the legitimization of a party label, and campaigns now cost more because candidates have to get their messages out without help from a party organization.

To increase minority representation and to cut campaign costs, some cities have returned to district elections. Los Angeles has used district elections since 1924; Sacramento converted in 1971, followed by San Jose, Oakland, and later San Diego and San Francisco. About two dozen California cities use district elections. Most cities that have reverted to district elections have done so through voter-approved charter amendments, but Watsonville, a small city near Monterey, did so under a 1988 federal court ruling that at-large elections prevented Latinos from winning representation on the city council even though they constituted nearly half the city's population.

Although district elections have increased opportunities for minority candidates in some cities, minorities remain substantially underrepresented overall in California local government. Latinos, Asians, and African Americans constitute more than 50 percent of the state's population, but respectively, they held only 20.7, 3.2, and 4.6 percent of its mayoral, city council, and county supervisor positions. Women have done somewhat better, with 36.9 percent. All these groups are more successful in local than in state elections, but they are still held back by discrimination, low participation, at-large elections, high campaign costs, and the lack of party support resulting from nonpartisan elections.

As with state-level campaigns, local reformers have been concerned about the costs of city and county races and the influence of money on politics. Between 1982 and 1992 alone, spending on local races in California increased by 1,300 percent.[1] Spending on local campaigns has continued to rise since then. Ninety-five California cities and counties have enacted local campaign finance laws that require disclosure of contributors and expenditures and sometimes limit the amount of contributions. Los Angeles restricts spending and provides limited public financing for campaigns. Nevertheless, in 2001, candidates for mayor of Los Angeles spent a combined total of more than $25 million in the primary and runoff elections; the winner, James Hahn, spent more than $7 million.

EXECUTIVE POWER

Because **mayors** were once connected with political machines, the Progressives stripped away their powers, shifting executive authority to council-appointed city managers who were intended to be neutral, professional administrators. Most California cities use this **council–manager system.** While the manager administers the city's programs, the council members alternate as mayor, a ceremonial post that involves chairing meetings and cutting ribbons.

San Francisco, however, uses a strong mayor form of government, in which the mayor is elected directly by the people to a four-year term and holds powers similar to those of the president in the national system, including the veto, budget control, and appointment of department heads. San Francisco Mayor Willie Brown, an African American, makes the most of these powers, as well as the spotlight that the office provides. Oakland switched to a strong mayor form of government in 1998, at the same time it elected former governor Jerry Brown its mayor.

Until recently, independent commissions ran most city departments, hiring department heads and overseeing their own budgets. But voters approved a new charter in 2000, enhancing the powers of the mayor by making department heads responsible to that office. Mayor James Hahn, elected in 2001, thus exercises more authority as mayor than any of his predecessors. In an effort to fend off the secession of discontented areas like the San Fernando Valley, the new charter also gave more power over land use and development decisions to neighborhoods.

Other California cities have moved away from the council–manager system of government. Some have kept their managers but have revised the system so that the mayor is directly elected, although he or she continues to sit as a council member without real executive power. Even without much authority, being a directly elected mayor brings visibility and influence. Mayors such as San Diego's Dick Murphy and San Jose's Ron Gonzales exercise substantial clout despite their limited official power.

California mayors will probably continue to grow stronger, partly because of media attention but also because of the genuine need for leadership in the growing tempest of city politics. Elected officials and community groups often complain about the lack of accountability inherent in the city manager form. "If people elect you to represent them," said Joe Serna, Jr., the late mayor of Sacramento, "and you're not given the power to hire and fire people, to make essential decisions, or to implement policies, it shows a certain disrespect for the voters. It says, 'You're not smart enough to choose your own representatives. We'd better bring in some professionals to get the job done.' The way things are right now, elected officials in this city have all the accountability and none of the responsibility."[2]

MORE GOVERNMENTS

Besides cities and counties, California has thousands of other, less visible local governments (Table 9.1). Created by the state or by citizens, they provide designated services and have taxing powers, mostly collecting their revenues as small portions of the property taxes paid by homeowners and businesses. Yet except for the school districts, most of us are unaware of their existence.

SCHOOL DISTRICTS AND SPECIAL DISTRICTS

In California, 984 local governments called **school districts** provide education. They are created and overseen by the state and governed by elected boards, which appoint professional educators as

TABLE 9.1
CALIFORNIA'S LOCAL GOVERNMENTS

TYPE	NUMBER
Counties	58
Cities	476
Redevelopment agencies	408
School districts	984
Special districts	4,792
TOTAL	6,718

SOURCE: California State Controller.

superintendents to oversee day-to-day operations. Except for parents and teachers, voter participation in school elections and politics is low, but with the future of their children at stake, their involvement is often intense. Recently, Christian fundamentalists have been particularly active in school politics.

The state supplies 54 percent of the funds for schools; most of the rest comes from local property taxes. This money is for operating expenses. Building repairs and construction of new schools are mostly funded for by bonds (borrowed money paid by local taxes), which until recently required approval by a two-thirds majority of the voters. Following the Proposition 13 tax revolt, such approvals became very rare, but in 2000, voters approved lowering the percentage required for approval to 55 percent and passing bonds became easier. School districts had begun winning voter approval even before the change, thanks in part to increasing reliance on professional campaign consultants.

Special districts are an even more common form of local government, with no fewer than 4,792 in California. Unlike cities and counties, which are "general-purpose" governments, special districts usually provide a single service. They are created when citizens or governments want a particular service performed but either have no appropriate government agency to perform the service or don't want to delegate it to a city or county. Sometimes special districts are formed when small communities share responsibilities for fire protection, sewage treatment, or other services that can be more efficiently provided on a larger scale. Small cities may rely on such special districts (or on counties and larger cities) to deliver the services that their citizens expect. Depending on the nature of the special district, funding usually is by property taxes or charges for the service that it provides. Altogether, California's special districts spend more than $16 billion a year–about half as much of all of California's cities.

A city council or a county board of supervisors governs some special districts, but a commission or board of directors, which may be elected or appointed by other officials, oversees most. Like a school board, this body usually appoints a professional administrator to manage its business. Accountability to the voters and taxpayers is a problem, however, because most of us aren't even aware of these officials. Few people know, for example, that the general manager of the Metropolitan Water District in Southern California is paid more than the governor.[3]

The use of special districts rose when Proposition 13 imposed tax constraints on general-purpose local governments. Some services can be more readily funded in this way. Thousands of common interest developments (CIDs) and business improvement districts (BIDs) have also been created. CIDs usually function in condominium or other housing developments and charge residents fees for services; BIDs operate in business areas and may charge fees or levy taxes as assessment districts. Both offer an alternative way of funding services, but only for some parts of communities. Boards selected by fee payers govern both.

Similarly, **redevelopment agencies** have proliferated since Proposition 13 as a way for cities to raise money for special purposes without voter action. California's 408 redevelopment agencies operate within cities to provide infrastructure and subsidies for new developments in areas designated as "blighted" (usually old city centers and industrial areas). New property tax revenues generated by redevelopment must be reinvested in the redevelopment areas, enabling cities to make infrastructure improvements and build public facilities such as convention centers and arenas. As with special districts, accountability is a problem with redevelopment agencies. Although such agencies are technically separate from city government, the local city council generally acts as the agency board of directors, but this is not the role for which council members are elected, nor is it often discussed in campaigns. Critics also charge that redevelopment agencies divert taxes from other services and hurt the low-income and minority residents of areas that are designated as "blighted."

REGIONAL GOVERNMENTS

The existence of so many sorts of local governments means that many operate in urbanized parts of California. The vast urban areas between Los Angeles and San Diego or San Francisco and San Jose, for example, consist of many cities, counties, and special districts, with no single authority in charge of the whole area. This fragmentation provides small-scale governments that are accessible to their citizens, but these governments are sometimes too small to provide needed services efficiently. In addition, problems such as transportation and air pollution go far beyond the boundaries of any one entity. Regional leaders in the Los

Angeles area fear that the secession movements there will only exacerbate this fragmentation, whereas the secessionists already think their local government is too large to be responsive.

Many California cities deal with this situation by contracting for services from counties, larger cities, or private businesses. The eighty-eight cities of Los Angeles County, for example, may pay the county to provide any of fifty-eight different services, from dog catching to tree planting. Small cities commonly contract with the county sheriff for police protection rather than fund their own forces. Contracting allows such communities to provide needed services while retaining local control, although some see the system as unfair because wealthy communities can afford more than poor ones.

Special districts are another way to deal with regional problems, particularly those extending beyond the boundaries of existing cities or counties, such as air pollution and transportation. California has forty-seven transit districts, for example, which run bus and rail systems. Most are countywide, but some, such as the Bay Area Rapid Transit (BART) system, cover several counties.

Twenty of California's urban areas also have **councils of government (COGs),** where all the cities and counties in each area are represented. The biggest COGs are the six-county Association of Southern California Governments (ASCG) and the nine-county Association of Bay Area Governments (ABAG) in Northern California. These regional bodies focus on land use planning and development, but because they cannot force their plans on local governments, they serve mainly as forums for communication and coordination among the jurisdictions they encompass.

As regional problems have grown and competition among cities has increased, the need for regional planning has also grown. The state has already used its authority over local governments to require the implementation of regional plans through agencies such as ABAG and ASCG. Other state-created agencies, such as the Metropolitan Water District and the South Coast Air Quality Management Board in Southern California, exercise great power. Environmentalists, big business, and metropolitan newspapers often advocate the creation of regional governments with the ability to deal with areawide issues such as transportation, air quality, and growth, but existing cities firmly oppose any loss of local control.

DIRECT DEMOCRACY IN LOCAL POLITICS

Direct democracy is used even more in local than in statewide politics. All charter changes, such as increasing the powers of the mayor or introducing district council elections, are subject to voter approval by referendum. Voters must also approve proposals for local governments to introduce or raise taxes or to borrow money by issuing bonds. Charter changes and general-purpose taxes require a simple majority, but a supermajority of two-thirds is required for taxes for a special purpose, such as for transportation. Imposed by voters in a series of statewide initiatives, these requirements have severely restricted the ability of local governments to raise money because voter approval is difficult to win. A 2000 initiative, however, made it a little easier for school districts to win voter approval of bond measures for new construction by lowering the required voter approval from 67 to 55 percent.

Local governments can place tax measures and charter amendments on the ballot, but citizens can also put proposals to the voters through the initiative process. Citizens have commonly done so to control growth and amend charters. District elections were introduced in some cities by initiative, as were **term limits,** usually restricting elected officials to two four-year terms. Several California counties and about forty cities now limit the terms of elected officials. As a last resort, voters may express their dissatisfaction with elected officials through recall elections. Recalls are rare, occurring mostly in school districts, but in 1999 voters in the heavily Latino Los Angeles suburb of Bell Gardens recalled three council members accused of corruption.

LAND USE: COPING WITH GROWTH

Perhaps the most frequent use of direct democracy in California cities and counties is by citizens seeking to control growth. Deciding how land can be used is a major power assigned to local governments by the state. The way they use this power affects us all. If they encourage growth in the form of housing, industry, or shopping centers, for example, the economy may boom, but streets may become clogged, schools overcrowded, sewage treatment plants strained, and police and fire protection stretched too thin. When this happens, environmentalists or residents who expect adequate services may grow frustrated and demand controls on growth. If the city council or county board of supervisors is unresponsive, they may take their case to the voters through an initiative.

Since 1971, when development became the state's predominant local issue, 90 percent of California communities have enacted some form of growth control, and sixty-three growth-related measures were on local ballots in November 2000. Several communities in fast-growing Ventura County have recently approved strict controls. The battle typically pits a grassroots coalition with little money against big-spending developers and builders. The antigrowth faction usually wins, but sometimes those who favor development have persuasively emphasized the economic benefits of growth, including jobs and housing. Voters in Orange County, Riverside County, and San Diego recently rejected growth-control measures, despite dissatisfaction with the local quality of life. Statewide surveys report that voter support for local growth control initiatives has declined from 58 percent in 2000 to 49 percent in 2002.[4]

TAXING AND SPENDING

The way that local governments raise and spend money reveals a great deal, not only about what they do but also about the limits they face in doing it.

The biggest single source of money for California's local governments used to be the **property tax,** an annual assessment based on the value of land and buildings. Then in 1978 the voters approved **Proposition 13,** a statewide initiative that cut property tax revenues by 57 percent. Cities adjusted to Proposition 13 in a variety of ways. Some cut jobs and services to save money. Many introduced or increased **charges for services** such as sewage treatment, trash collection, building permits, and the use of recreational facilities. Such charges are now the largest source of income for most cities (Figure 9.3), followed by the **sales tax,** which returns 1.5 percent of the state's basic 7.25 percent tax to the city where the sale occurred (or the county, in the case of unincorporated areas). Utility taxes also help some cities, such as San Jose, where they generate 9 percent of local revenues, almost as much as property taxes. The shift from property taxes to other sources of revenue also affected local land use decisions. When a new development is proposed, most cities now prefer retail businesses to housing or industry because of the sales taxes such businesses generate. This has been labeled the **fiscalization of land use** because instead of choosing the best use for the land, cities opt for the one that produces the most revenue.

With more legal constraints on their taxing powers, counties had an even rougher time after Proposition 13. State aid to counties increased slightly, with an extra 1.25 percent of the state sales tax set aside for counties to spend on health, public safety, and transportation. (Some counties also levy an additional local sales tax for transportation.) But with no alternative local taxes readily available after the passage of Proposition 13, most counties cut spending deeply. Years later they are still struggling to provide essential services, a struggle that intensified after the legislature and governor shifted billions of dollars from counties to schools in the budget crises of the 1990s.

More than half of county revenues come from the state and federal governments (40 percent and 22 percent, respectively), but this money

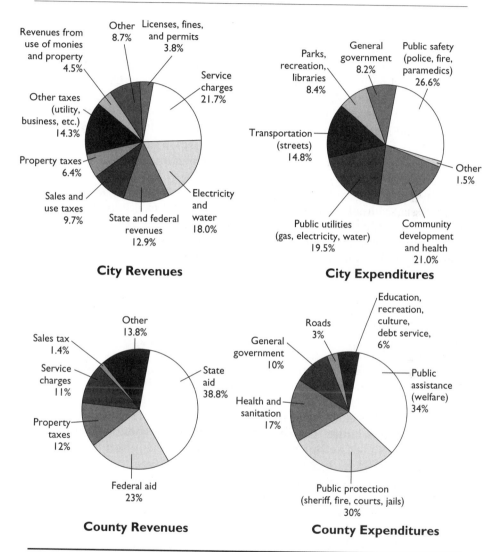

FIGURE 9.3

REVENUES AND EXPENDITURES OF CALIFORNIA CITIES AND COUNTIES, 1999–2000

City Revenues

Other 8.7%
Licenses, fines, and permits 3.8%
Revenues from use of monies and property 4.5%
Service charges 21.7%
Other taxes (utility, business, etc.) 14.3%
Property taxes 6.4%
Sales and use taxes 9.7%
State and federal revenues 12.9%
Electricity and water 18.0%

City Expenditures

Parks, recreation, libraries 8.4%
General government 8.2%
Public safety (police, fire, paramedics) 26.6%
Transportation (streets) 14.8%
Other 1.5%
Public utilities (gas, electricity, water) 19.5%
Community development and health 21.0%

County Revenues

Other 13.8%
Sales tax 1.4%
Service charges 11%
Property taxes 12%
State aid 38.8%
Federal aid 23%

County Expenditures

Roads 3%
General government 10%
Education, recreation, culture, debt service, 6%
Public assistance (welfare) 34%
Health and sanitation 17%
Public protection (sheriff, fire, courts, jails) 30%

SOURCE: California State Controller, 2002.

must be spent on required programs and institutions such as welfare, medical assistance, and the courts. Even so, state and federal aid does not cover the cost of these mandatory services, leaving counties with little money to spend as they choose. The average California county now spends 95 percent of its funds on state-mandated services, compared with 70 percent fifteen years ago.[5]

Counties have responded to these constraints in a variety of ways. Like cities, most counties have increased charges and fees for services. Orange County, for example, approved California's first toll road in half a century when it couldn't afford to build a new freeway. Orange County was also nearly bankrupted when its county treasurer tried to make money for the county by using funds on hand to play the stock market and instead lost disastrously. The county's conservative voters rejected a modest tax increase to compensate for the losses, opting instead for drastic cuts in services and shifting money out of transportation and other special funds.

Just as revenue sources vary among cities and counties, so do spending patterns, largely because the state assigns them different responsibilities. Spending also varies because some cities take on services provided elsewhere by counties. As shown in Figure 9.3, public safety is the biggest expenditure for California cities, whereas welfare is the biggest county expenditure.

LOCAL LIMITS

California's political system gives residents of cities and counties many opportunities to decide what sort of communities they want, and Californians have made good use of these opportunities. But the state also limits what can be done at the local level, as Proposition 13 and ongoing budget battles clearly show. Some may dispute such intervention, but the state's authority remains supreme.

Notes

1. *The Book of the States 1992–1993*, vol. 29, Lexington, KY: Council of State Governments, 1992, p. 288.
2. Ed Goldman, "Out of the Sandbox," *California Journal*, May 1993, p. 16.
3. In 2002 the general manager of the Metropolitan Water District earned $275,000; the governor was paid $175,000 as of December 2002.
4. *PPIC Statewide Survey*, San Francisco: Public Policy Institute of California, March 2000 and June 2002, www.ppic.org.
5. County Supervisors Association of California.

Learn More on the World Wide Web

Association of (San Francisco) Bay Area Governments: www.abag.org

Cities: www.cacities.org

Counties: www.csac.counties.org

Public Policy Institute of California (studies on local tax sources): www.ppic.org

Southern California Association of Governments: www.scag.org

Learn More at the Library

Jeffrey I. Chapman, *Proposition 13: Some Unintended Consequences,* San Francisco: Public Policy Institute of California, 1998.

Paul G. Lewis, *Deep Roots: Local Government Structure in California,* San Francisco: Public Policy Institute of California, 1998.

Peter Schrag, *Paradise Lost,* Berkeley: University of California Press, 1999.

Randy Shilts, *The Mayor of Castro Street,* New York: St. Martin's, 1982.

CHAPTER 10

STATE-FEDERAL RELATIONS: CONFLICT, COOPERATION, AND CHAOS

Part of California's uniqueness stems from its position as the nation's most populated state; part also stems from the state's vast resources and size. Problems and achievements occur in proportions here that are unequaled elsewhere. And so it is regarding the state's relationship with the federal government.

Sometimes state and national leaders differ in opinion about how California should be managed. Environmental protection and government regulation of power prices are two such thorny policy areas. On other issues, such as workplace conditions and foreign trade, the two governments have worked well together. Deciding the best responses to problems that impact both the nation and state can be a challenge because, like its forty-nine counterparts, California is both a self-governing state and member of the larger national government.

Matters become even more complicated when attempts are made to determine financial responsibility for new highways, immigration control, or endangered species protection, to name a few. Because the state is so large and complex, federal assistance almost always seems inadequate. Yet, when federal aid or programs are cut, California seems to suffer disproportionately.

Nevertheless, when the state succeeds, its attainment is often the harbinger of similar good fortune destined to reach the rest of the nation. The right-to-choose movement, environmentalism, political reform, and the tax revolt all had early beginnings—and in some cases, origins—in California.

In this chapter we review California's impact on national policymaking, especially with respect to the state's leverage in Congress. We also explore some of the critical policy areas that test California's relationship with the federal government: immigration, the environment, and the distribution of federal resources to the state of California. Each issue touches on the delicate balance between state autonomy and national objectives–perspectives that are not always shared. These issues are important not only because of their present urgency, but also because of their effects on California's people, economy, and political values.

CALIFORNIA'S CLOUT IN WASHINGTON

In congressional politics, the majority political party in each house controls the committee chairs, which, in turn, control the flow of legislation. Seniority is key to gaining chairmanships in Congress, but the relatively low seniority of Californian Republicans has kept the state's Republican members from climbing the leadership ladder. In fact, since 1995, California Republicans have never chaired more than two committees and have chaired only one committee in 2002.[1] At the same time, Ohio and Florida each had three of the twenty chairmanships in the House of Representatives. All this has occurred even though as of 2003, California has fifty-three members, dwarfing those of every other state; Texas and New York are second and third, with thirty-one and thirty members, respectively. On the Democratic side, in 2002 San Francisco Congresswoman Nancy Pelosi won election to the post of Democratic Minority Leader, the highest national leadership position ever held by a woman.

Matters are somewhat different in the U.S. Senate. Although the upper house is a bit less partisan than the lower house, the majority party still controls all committees. Democrats have held a slim majority in 2001, but Republicans resumed control after the 2002 elections. California's two Democratic Senators, Dianne Feinstein and Barbara Boxer, lack sufficient seniority to hold chairmanships, but they have exercised considerable influence over issues such as energy, judicial appointments, and environmental policy.

INTERNAL COMPOSITION

In many respects California's congressional makeup is as diverse as the rest of the state. As of 2003, the fifty-three-member House delegation includes eight Latinos, four African Americans, and two Asians; eighteen women are members of the delegation. Both of California's U.S. senators are women as well.

Unlike the overall composition of the House of Representatives, Democrats in California now enjoy a comfortable margin of 33–20 over Republicans. The reelection of Democrat Dianne Feinstein to the U.S. Senate in 2000 kept both of the state's senate seats in the Democratic camp, contrary to the national Republican majority.

DIVISIVENESS

One other fact must be added to the discussion of Californians in Washington—historically, the state's congressional delegation has been notoriously fractured in its responses to key public policy issues affecting California. Much of the differences in behavior stems from the make up of their districts. North/south, urban/rural, and coastal/valley/mountain divisions separate the state geographically. Other differences exist, too, in terms of wealth, ethnicity, and basic liberal/conservative distinctions. To be sure, no congressional district is completely homogenous, yet most members of Congress tend to protect their districts' turf more than the state as a whole. Thus, on issues ranging from desert protection to immigration, representatives often have canceled each other's votes, leaving states such as Texas far more powerful because of their relatively unified stances. Even on foreign trade issues, members from California often have worked at cross-purposes, depending on the industries, interest groups, and demographic characteristics that affect their districts. Only on the question of offshore oil drilling have most members of the state's delegation voted the same way.

The struggle over the proposed Auburn Dam is a current case in point. The massive $2 billion proposal has been considered in Congress since 1960, yet California lawmakers in Washington have remained paralyzed over the issue. Republican John Doolittle, chair of the House Subcommittee on Power and Resources, and Sacramento Democrat Bob Matsui have pushed the project, but Democrats Pete Stark and George Miller have adamantly opposed it. The issue of whether the project is a boondoggle or a necessary flood control program is not as significant as the fact that it has polarized California members of the House of Representatives. As a result, while Californians have fussed among themselves over this polarizing question, representatives from other states have worked in bipartisan ways to garner federal dollars.

TERRORISM

September 11, 2001, represented a turning point in American history. Never before had terrorists penetrated American soil in such a punishing way. As expected, the federal government took the lead in responding to this unprecedented event. With passage of the USA Patriot Act on October 26, 2001, the national government assumed expanded powers to search out terrorism and terrorist-related activities in the areas of hazardous substances, money laundering, illegal immigration, cybercrime, fraud, and other related areas. Acting in concert with these new powers, U.S. Attorney General John Ashcroft asked the states and local governments to help in the detaining and questioning of suspicious persons, the new Transportation Security Administration assumed security responsibilities at the nation's airports, and the U.S. Border Patrol increased its vigilance against illegal entry.

Although the federal government has picked up much of the tab, the states have been burdened with significant costs, too, and are likely to see those costs continue well into the future. From bus transportation systems to water transportation conduits, California's infrastructure will require additional protection from terror. In Los Angeles, for example, Mayor James Hahn has proposed a $9.6 billion plan to improve security at Los Angeles International Airport, the nation's fourth busiest facility.[2] Statewide, California Highway Patrol Commissioner D. O. "Spike" Helmick has estimated that local law enforcement costs would increase by a staggering $2 billion.[3] Such costs are difficult for governments to swallow in good economic times, but with the state plagued by a lingering recession throughout 2002 and into 2003, they are sure to make a dent in the struggle over depleted state resources.

IMMIGRATION

California has long been a magnet for those in search of opportunity. And they have come–first the Spanish, then the Yankees, the Irish, and the Chinese during the nineteenth century, followed by Japanese, Eastern Europeans, African Americans, and more Latinos during the first three-fourths of the twentieth century. But over the past two decades, several independent events have converged to influence the moods of the state's residents and would-be residents. Lack of opportunity in other nations has led millions to choose California as an alternative; meanwhile, a burdened and underfunded infrastructure has led many of those already here to oppose further immigration. Much of the antipathy has been directed at Latinos, but anger has also been aimed at Asians.

The numbers involved are substantial. Whereas 15.1 percent of California's population was foreign-born in 1980, 26.2 percent fell within that category in 2000. During the same period the percentage of foreign-born occupants of the United States as a whole edged up from 6.2 to 9.7 (Figure 10.1). Between 1990 and 1999, California's population grew by between 500,000 and 600,000 annually, more than 40 percent of whom came from foreign immigration. In 2000 the federal government's Census Bureau estimated that there were 7.5 million illegal immigrants nationwide, with at least 3 million of them in California.

As these dramatic events began to reshape California, experts argued about whether the immigrants helped or harmed the state's economy. One study claimed that within a three-month period, immigrants–legal

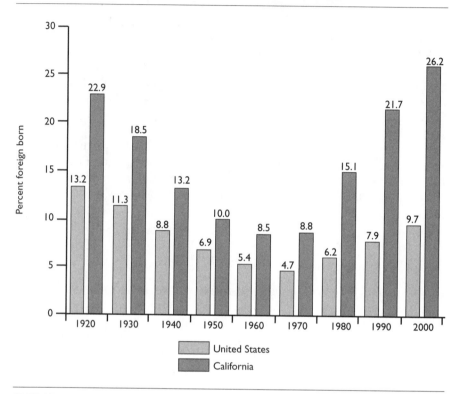

FIGURE 10.1

POPULATION OF FOREIGN-BORN RESIDENTS, CALIFORNIA AND UNITED STATES COMPARED

SOURCE: U.S. Bureau of Census.

and illegal—cost the state $18 billion in services; another study countered that immigrants—legal and illegal—contributed a net increase of $12 billion in taxes to California's economy.[4] These studies underscore the anguish and confusion associated with the immigration issue.

Opponents of illegal immigration achieved statewide success in November 1994 with the passage of **Proposition 187,** an initiative that prohibited illegal immigrants from collecting welfare, receiving government-financed medical care, and attending public schools. Adversaries of the measure characterized it as immigrant-bashing and as little more than a convenient way to avoid discussing the state's true problems, whereas proponents described it as an overdue response to a critical problem. In 1998 a U.S. federal district court judge ruled that most provisions of the act were unconstitutional.

AFFIRMATIVE ACTION AND DISCRIMINATION

The essence of **affirmative action** lies in the ability of a government entity to ensure that groups historically victimized by discrimination are able to compete for government jobs and public university admissions on a "level playing field" with others who have not suffered such histories. Affirmative action has been part of the national landscape since 1965, when it was established as an executive order of President Lyndon Johnson. In the three decades following its creation, the concept has been molded by the U.S. Congress and clarified in a series of rulings by the federal courts. Typically, affirmative action has been applied most to nonwhites and females.

During the Wilson administration, affirmative action became a contentious issue in California. Arguing that it was unfair, and actually pitting some groups against others, the governor repeatedly demanded without success that the legislature end all state affirmative action programs. In 1995 Wilson used his executive order authority to eliminate affirmative action in any state agencies and boards not designated by the legislature or national government. In 1996 the governor campaigned for **Proposition 209,** an initiative promising to do away with affirmative action programs based on race or gender. Passed by a comfortable 54 to 46 percent margin in November 1996, the initiative put the state on a collision course with a spate of recent national laws and court decisions. Nevertheless, in 1997 the U.S. Supreme Court upheld the proposition, signaling a more conservative interpretation of affirmative action in California and throughout the nation.

For Governor Wilson, the U.S. Supreme Court decision gave him a rare victory in his many struggles with the federal government. For the University of California, implementation of the initiative has led to the admission of fewer African American and Latino students. Nevertheless, the federal government and many private-sector entities have continued to rely on affirmative action guidelines for employment and contract programs.[5]

AIR POLLUTION

Some public policies in California result more from federal pressure than from state will. No example is more obvious than environmental protection, particularly as it pertains to clean air. According to the 1990 Clean Air Act amendments, five of the seven most polluted areas in the entire country lie in California; nevertheless, considerable opposition to antipollution activity has existed because of the massive costs associated with environmental repair and fears that those costs would lead to economic disaster. This dilemma has pitted Californians against Washington, D.C., and also against each other, especially Northern versus Southern California interests.

The road to consensus has been bumpy, in part because the state of California and the federal government each claim jurisdiction over air and water. At times the federal government has deferred to requests from the state of California because of pleas that federal standards would strangle Southern California companies as well as their automobile-dependent workforce. At other times the federal government's **Environmental Protection Agency** (EPA) has urged, prodded, and threatened the state into compliance with respect to fundamental national objectives. At other times still, the federal government has discouraged the state from innovation, such as in 2002, when the Bush administration joined in a suit to keep California from imposing auto emissions standards stronger than other states.

Nowhere have the choices been more difficult than with air pollution in Southern California, the home to much of the state's pollution-emitting industry and dirty air. For years the South Coast Air Quality Management District, California's major environmental agency in the area, has struggled to enforce federal rules without harming the economy. Although emissions have been reduced considerably by the agency, they must be pared by another 60 percent before 2010 to comply with federal standards. Failure to meet this deadline will result in huge federal fines and the possible shutdown of local industries. In 1999 business representatives and the state and the federal government agreed on twelve rules for businesses to eliminate as much as forty-eight tons of pollution per day. In 2002 the EPA and state came to terms on a plan to reduce vehicle smog emissions, thereby freeing $716 million of federal aid for highway projects that had been frozen during the dispute.[6]

Matters have not been resolved as easily in the Central Valley, however. In 2002 the EPA announced an end to an exemption for California farmers who had been allowed to operate heavy farm machinery outside of the emissions rules. The EPA took the new stand because of the extraordinarily high percentages of children in the area suffering from asthma, thought to be caused by the area's growing air pollution. Farmer groups claimed that they would be forced out of business, whereas health organizations hailed the decision.[7]

Along the winding road to environmentalism, the state has invented necessary compromises, such as a "smog exchange" program that would allow polluters to "buy" sulfur oxides, hydrocarbons, and other emissions from those companies that stay below their allowed pollution levels. This law drew the wrath of environmentalists. In 2002 California legislators also passed landmark legislation requiring automakers to significantly reduce greenhouse gasses from cars, trucks, minivans, and sport-utility vehicles by 2009. This law drew the wrath of businesses. Simply put, there is no easy way for the state to deal with the air pollution issue.

WATER

Not all of California's jurisdictional disputes have occurred with the federal government. In several areas the state has tangled with other states. The storage of nuclear waste and agriculture rules are two such examples of state fights. But no argument has as much significance as California's struggle for fresh water. Given the state's huge population and pivotal role in agriculture, water is a resource California can ill-afford to do without.

The lynchpin of the water struggle dispute between California and other states is the Colorado River, the fresh water source that begins in Colorado and winds through six other states. Under a 1922 multistate agreement, California is entitled to 4.4 million-acre feet, or 59 percent, of the lower basin river annually. Yet according to some critics, California has exceeded its share by as much as 1 million acre-feet per year,[8] a condition that has become problematic with dramatic population growth in Arizona and Nevada.

Fearing an all-out water war that would spill into Congress, officials from seven states held talks for eighteen months to resolve the problem. In 2000 they agreed to a formula that would allow California to gradually reduce consumption of the excess over a fifteen-year period. During the transition, officials from Arizona have offered to "bank" surplus water for California, should the state require it. At least for the time being, the seven western states have solved a thorny issue without federal participation.

Meanwhile, the federal government's Department of Interior and the state worked to resolve for a time the ongoing battle among agribusiness, which uses 79 percent of the state's water; environmentalists seeking to preserve rivers and deltas; and urban areas in need of water to grow. Under the auspices of CalFed, a joint federal and state water agency, the two governments in 2000 developed a plan to expand existing federal reservoirs located in California, improve drinking water quality, and develop a creative water recycling program. Most of the $8.5 billion price tag will be borne by the federal government.

SHARED RESOURCES

The word **federalism** refers to the multifaceted political relationship that binds the state and national governments. One aspect of that relationship centers on financial assistance that wends its way from federal coffers to state treasuries. The preponderance of this assistance comes in the form of **grants-in-aid,** amounting to more than $293 billion in 2000 and, on average, amounting to about 22 percent of all state and local government revenues. This assistance is the result of more than 500 federal programs designed to assist states in areas ranging from agricultural development to high-tech research. For decades California received more than its fair share of grants-in-aid from the federal government. With defense- and space-related research serving as a huge economic magnet, the Golden State received more money from the federal government than it sent in.

That has changed. In 1981 California had 10 percent of the national population but received 15 percent of the national government's expenditures. By 1983 the federal share had jumped to 22 percent. Then came the slide. With a pared defense budget, cutbacks in infrastructure work, and the push for a balanced budget, federal contributions have shrunk considerably. As of 2001 California had 12.5 percent of the nation's population but received 11 percent of the nation's federal funds. The state now ranks fortieth on a per capita basis among federal grant-in-aid recipients, down sharply from twentieth in 1990.[9]

There is another way to appreciate the changing relationship between the federal government and California. Because of the state's massive growth and receipt of federal assistance in highway and water projects and environmental protection, California has had a history of getting more dollars from the federal government than it contributes. Beginning in 1986, however, California became a "donor" state, as depicted in Figure 10.2. As a result, for the past decade, California has contributed more money to the national treasury than it has received. Thus, in 2000, for every dollar sent from California to Washington, D.C., the state received eighty-eight cents in federal goods and services.

The data presented here fly in the face of the political posturing that has emerged from both Congress and the presidency in recent years. They are also a reflection of the fragmentation that has haunted the state's congressional delegation on virtually every issue except offshore oil drilling. As a result, California's "Golden State" nickname has a different meaning in Washington than in California—namely, sizable economic resources that have landed disproportionately in the federal treasury.

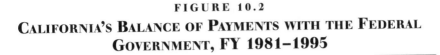

FIGURE 10.2

CALIFORNIA'S BALANCE OF PAYMENTS WITH THE FEDERAL
GOVERNMENT, FY 1981–1995

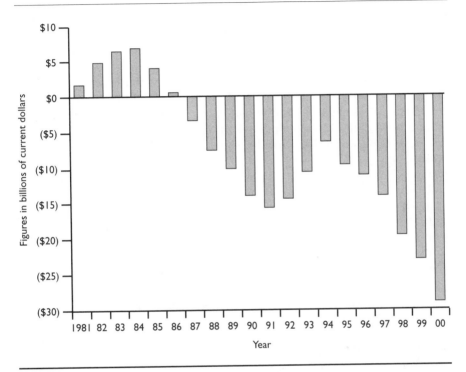

SOURCES: U.S. Census Bureau and Tax Foundation.

CHANGED RULES, NEW DIRECTIONS

As national leaders have altered the course of U.S. politics and public
policies, their efforts have been felt profoundly in California. The state's
fragmented congressional delegation and a Republican-led Congress
have only exacerbated California's inability to be heard.

Whereas the Congress in recent years has had something of an
"arm's length" relationship with California, Democratic President Bill
Clinton embraced the state. Keenly aware of the state's growing wealth
and the value of California's fifty-four electoral votes (20 percent of
the Electoral College votes needed to win the presidency), he funneled

discretionary funds to California, particularly in the areas of high-tech research and defense industry projects. None of this was lost on the California electorate, who supported Democratic Vice President Al Gore in 2000 over winner Republican George W. Bush.

During the first half of his four-year term, Bush has not tended to California with the zeal of his predecessor. To the contrary, the Bush administration ignored California when the state sought relief from the Federal Regulatory Energy Commission over excessive electricity prices in 2001. Other fights have occurred over air pollution, agriculture, and international trade. And still unresolved is the extent to which the federal government will help California with its bills for fighting terrorism.

Presidential elections notwithstanding, California has been weaned from a good deal of its dependence on federal dollars. The process may not have been enjoyable, but the state now is more diversified for the effort.

Notes

1. The one House Republican committee chair from California was William Thomas (House Ways and Means Committee).
2. "$9.6 Billion Make-Over for LAX?," *Los Angeles Times*, July 2, 2002, pp. A1, A17.
3. "Mounting Costs Worry Safety Agencies," *Sacramento Bee*, November 16, 2001, p. 1A.
4. "1992 Cost of Immigrants $18 Billion, Report Says," *Los Angeles Times*, November 5, 1993, pp. A3, A31; and "Immigrants Found a Fiscal Plus," *Los Angeles Times*, February 23, 1994, p. B4.
5. See "Acceptance of Blacks, Latinos to UC Plunges," *Los Angeles Times*, April 1, 1998, pp. A1, A20; and "Despite Wilson Order, Goals for Diversity Thrive Elsewhere," *Los Angeles Times*, March 13, 1998, pp. A1, A19.
6. "EPA Accepts Bay Area Smog Plans," *San Francisco Chronicle*, July 15, 2002, pp. A23.
7. "U.S. Plans to End Exemption of California Farmers From Air Pollution Standards," *The New York Times*, May 15, 2002, p. A15.
8. "Western States Blast California Over Water Use," *Las Vegas Review-Journal*, May 22, 1999, p. 5b. The six states in addition to California are Arizona, Colorado, Nevada, New Mexico, Utah, and Wyoming.
9. Institute for Federal Policy Research, "California's Balance of Payments with the Federal Treasury, 1981–2000," April 2002.

Learn More on the World Wide Web

California and federal taxes: www.taxfoundation.org

California taxes: www.caltax.org

Environmental Protection Agency: www.epa.gov

Immigration: www.ccir.net; www.irps.ucsd.edu

Sierra Club: www.sierraclub.org

U.S. House of Representatives: www.house.gov

U.S. Senate: www.senate.gov

Learn More at the Library

Mark Baldassare, *Statewide Survey,* Public Policy Institute of California, www.ppic.org.

Gary C. Bryner, *Blue Skies, Green Politics,* 2nd ed., Washington, DC: CQ Press, 1995.

John Isbister, *The Immigration Debate,* West Hartford, CT: Kumarian Press, 1996.

GLOSSARY

affirmative action Public policy that avails groups with histories of discrimination the opportunity to compete for government jobs and public university admissions on an equal basis with others; state programs eliminated by California voters in 1996.

at-large elections Local elections in which all candidates are elected by the community as a whole rather than by districts.

attorney general California's top law enforcement officer and legal counsel; second most powerful member of the executive branch.

bank and corporation tax Tax on the profits of lending institutions and businesses; third most important source of state revenue.

bicameral legislature Organization of the state legislature into two houses, the forty-member senate (elected for four-year terms) and the eighty-member assembly (elected for two-year terms).

Big Five The governor, assembly speaker, assembly minority leader, senate president pro tem, and senate minority leader, who together share responsibility for making major decisions pertaining to the annual budget.

blanket primary A voter-approved nominating election system (1996) that allowed all registered voters to participate in the primary nominations of their choice, regardless of their party affiliation; declared unconstitutional by the U.S. Supreme Court in 2000.

Board of Equalization Five-member state board that oversees the collection of sales, gasoline, and liquor taxes; members elected by district; part of the executive branch.

board of supervisors Five-member governing body of counties, usually elected by district to four-year terms.

central committees Political party organizations at county and state levels; weakly linked to one another.

charges for services Local government fees for services such as sewage treatment, trash collection, building permits, and the use of recreational facilities; a major source of income for cities and counties since passage of Proposition 13 in 1978.

charter A document defining the powers and institutions of a California city or county.

cities Local governments in urban areas, run by city councils and mayors or city managers; principal responsibilities include police and fire protection, land use planning, street maintenance and construction, sanitation, libraries, and parks.

city councils Governing bodies of cities; members elected at-large or by district to four-year terms.

city manager Top administrative officer in most California cities; appointed by the city council.

civil service System for hiring and retaining public employees on the basis of their qualifications or merit; replaced the political machine's patronage, or spoils, system; encompasses 98 percent of state workers.

closed primary Election of party nominees in which only party members may participate.

collegiality Deferential behavior among justices as a way of building consensus on issues before the court.

Commission on Judicial Appointments Commission to review the governor's nominees for appellate and supreme courts; consists of the attorney general, the chief justice of the state supreme court, and the senior presiding judge of the courts of appeal.

Commission on Judicial Performance State board empowered to investigate charges of judicial misconduct or incompetence.

conference committee Committee of senate and assembly members that meets to reconcile different versions of the same bill.

contract lobbyist Individual or company that represents the interests of clients before the legislature and other policymaking entities.

controller Independently elected state executive who oversees taxing and spending.

council–manager system Form of government in which an elected council appoints a professional manager to administer daily operations; used by most California cities.

councils of government (COGs) Regional planning organizations.

counties Local governments and administrative agencies of the state, run by elected boards of supervisors; principal responsibilities include welfare, jails, courts, roads, and elections.

county executive Top administrative officer in most California counties; appointed by board of supervisors.

courts of appeal Three-justice panels that hear appeals from lower courts.

cross-filing Election system that allowed candidates to win the nomination of more than one political party; eliminated in 1959.

demographic groups Interest groups based on race, ethnicity, gender, or age; usually concerned with overcoming discrimination.

direct democracy Progressive reforms giving citizens the power to make and repeal laws (initiative and referendum) and to remove elected officials from office (recall).

direct mail Modern campaign technique by which candidates communicate selected messages to selected voters by mail.

director of finance State officer primarily responsible for preparation of the budget; appointed by the governor.

district attorney Chief prosecuting officer elected in each county; represents the people in cases against the accused.

district elections Elections in which candidates are chosen by only one part of the city, county, or state.

Environmental Protection Agency Federal government body charged with carrying out national environmental policy objectives.

Fair Political Practices Commission (FPPC) Established by the Political Reform Act of 1974, this independent regulatory commission monitors candidate campaign finance reports and lobbyists.

federalism The distribution of power, resources, and responsibilities among the national, state, and local governments.

fiscalization of land use When making land use decisions, cities opt for the alternative that produces the most revenue.

general election Statewide election held on the first Tuesday after the first Monday of November in even-numbered years.

general law city or county A city or county whose powers and structure of government are derived from state law.

general veto Gubernatorial power to reject an entire bill or budget; overruled only by an absolute two-thirds vote of both legislative houses.

governor California's highest-ranking executive; elected every four years.

grants-in-aid Payments from the national government to states to assist fulfillment of public policy objectives.

incorporation Process by which residents of an urbanized area form a city.

independent expenditures Campaign spending by interest groups and political action committees on behalf of candidates.

initiative Progressive device by which people may put laws and constitutional amendments on the ballot after securing enough voters' signatures.

insurance commissioner Elected state executive who regulates the insurance industry; created by 1988 initiative.

interest groups Nongovernmental organizations of individuals with similar concerns who seek to influence public policy.

item veto Gubernatorial power to delete or reduce the budgets within a bill without rejecting the entire bill or budget; absolute two-thirds vote of both houses of the state legislature required to override.

Judicial Council Chaired by the chief justice of the state supreme court and composed of twenty-one judges and attorneys; makes the rules for court procedures, collects data on the courts' operations and workload, and gives seminars for judges.

legislative analyst Assistant to the legislature who studies the annual budget and proposed programs.

legislative committees Small groups of senators or assembly members who consider and make legislation in specialized areas, such as agriculture or education.

legislative counsel Assists the legislature in preparing bills and assessing their impact on existing legislation.

legislative initiatives Propositions placed on the ballot by the legislature rather than by initiative petition.

lieutenant governor Chief executive when the governor is absent from the state or disabled; succeeds the governor in case of death or other departure from office; casts a tie-breaking vote in the senate; independently elected.

litigation Interest group tactic of challenging a law or policy in the courts by seeking to have it overruled, modified, or delayed.

lobbying Interest group efforts to influence political decision makers, often through paid, professionals (lobbyists).

local agency formation commission (LAFCO) A county agency set up to oversee the creation and expansion of cities.

logrolling A give-and-take process in which legislators trade support for each other's bills.

mayor Ceremonial leader of a city, usually a position alternated among council members, but in some large cities directly elected and given substantial powers.

nonpartisan elections Progressive reform removing party labels from ballots for local and judicial offices.

personal income tax A graduated tax on individual earnings adopted in 1935; the largest source of state revenues.

plea bargaining Reaching an agreement between prosecution and the accused; the former gets a conviction, and the latter agrees to a reduced charge and lesser penalty.

political action committees (PACs) Mechanisms by which interest groups direct campaign contributions to preferred candidates.

Political Reform Act of 1974 Initiative requiring officials to disclose conflicts of interest, campaign contributions and spending, and requiring lobbyists to register.

preprimary endorsement Political parties designation of preferred candidates in party primary elections, thus strengthening the roles of party organizations in selecting candidates; banned by state law until 1990.

president pro tem Legislative leader of the state senate; chairs the Senate Rules Committee; selected by the majority party.

primary election Election to choose party nominees; held in March of even-numbered years.

Progressives Members of an antimachine reform movement that reshaped the state's political institutions between 1907 and the 1920s.

property tax A tax on land and buildings; until passage of Proposition 13 in 1978, the primary source of revenues for local governments.

Proposition 4 (Gann initiative) A 1979 ballot measure that placed a strict cap on public spending; modified by Proposition 111 in 1990.

Proposition 8 (Victims' Bill of Rights) A 1982 initiative extending prison terms and thus increasing California's prison population and expenditures.

Proposition 13 (Jarvis-Gann initiative) Property tax-cutting ballot measure of 1978.

Proposition 98 A 1988 initiative awarding public education a fixed percentage of the state budget.

Proposition 111 A 1990 initiative that increased fuel taxes and modified Proposition 4's spending limits.

Proposition 140 A 1990 initiative limiting assembly members to three two-year terms and senators and statewide elected officials to two four-year terms and cutting the legislature's budget.

Proposition 172 A 1993 referendum in which voters made permanent a half-cent sales tax addition earmarked for local government expenditure on public safety.

Proposition 187 A 1994 initiative reducing government benefits for illegal immigrants; declared unconstitutional by federal courts in 1995.

Proposition 209 A 1996 initiative that eliminated affirmative action in California.

Proposition 218 A 1996 initiative requiring voter approval on all increases in local government tax and fees; in some cases, only property owners may vote.

Proposition 227 A 1998 initiative limiting bilingual education to no more than one year.

public defender County officer who represents defendants who cannot afford an attorney; appointed by county board of supervisors.

public interest groups Organizations that purport to represent all the people rather than private interests.

reapportionment Adjustment of legislative district boundaries by the state legislature to keep all districts equal in population; done every ten years after the national census.

recall Progressive reform allowing voters to remove elected officials by petition and majority vote.

redevelopment agencies Local government agencies operating within and controlled by cities to provide infrastructure and subsidies for new commercial and industrial developments in areas designated as "blighted" (usually old city centers and industrial areas).

referendum Progressive reform requiring the legislature to place certain measures before the voters, who may also repeal legislation by petitioning for a referendum.

Reynolds v. Sims A 1964 U.S. Supreme Court decision that ordered redistricting of the upper houses of all state legislatures by population instead of land.

runoff election The top two candidates in a nonpartisan primary for trial court judge or local office face each other.

sales tax Statewide tax on most goods and products; adopted in 1933. Local governments receive a portion of this tax.

school districts Local governments created by states to provide elementary and secondary education; governed by elected school boards.

secretary of state Elected state executive who keeps records and supervises elections.

Senate Rules Committee Chief committee for assigning chairs and committee appointments; chaired by the senate president pro tem.

Serrano v. Priest A 1972 California Supreme Court case that struck down the property tax as the main source of education funding.

Silicon Valley Top area for high-tech industries; located between San Jose and San Francisco.

single-issue groups Organized groups with unusually narrow policy objectives; not oriented toward compromise.

Southern Pacific Railroad Railroad company founded in 1861; developed a political machine that dominated state politics through the turn of the century.

speaker of the assembly Legislative leader of the assembly; selected by the majority party; controls committee appointments and the legislative process.

special districts Local government agencies providing a single service, such as fire protection or sewage disposal.

state auditor Assistant to the legislature who analyzes ongoing programs.

superintendent of public instruction Elected state executive in charge of public education.

supreme court California's highest judicial body; hears appeals from lower courts.

term limits Limits on the number of terms that officeholders may serve; elected executive branch officers and state senators are limited to two four-year terms, and assembly members are limited to three two-year terms.

third parties Minor political parties that capture small percentages of the vote in the general election but are viewed as important protest vehicles.

"three strikes" A 1994 law and initiative requiring sentences of twenty-five years to life for anyone convicted of three felonies.

treasurer Elected state executive, responsible for state funds between collection and spending.

trial courts Lower courts in which civil and criminal cases are first tried.

user taxes Taxes on select commodities or services "used" by those who benefit directly from them.

veto See **general veto** and **item veto.**

Workingmen's party Denis Kearney's antirailroad, anti–Chinese organization; instrumental in rewriting California's constitution in 1879.

INDEX

Absentee ballots, 28
Affirmative action, 127
    elimination of, 86, 127
African Americans
    city offices occupied by, 112
    immigration, 6
    median household income, 13
    state offices occupied by, 29
    voters, 28
Agencies of the state, 84–85. *See also* Local
    government
Agribusiness
    history of, 3
    interest groups, 42
    today, 9, 10
Aid to Families with Dependent Children (AFDC), 104
Air pollution, 127–129
Alcohol tax, 97
American Association of Retired Persons (AARP), 43
American Electronics Association, 42
American Indians. *See* Native Americans
Amnesty for illegal aliens, 8
Angelides, Phil, 90
Annexation powers of cities, 109
Appeal of judicial decisions, 68, 71–72
Appellate courts. *See* Courts of Appeal; Supreme
    Court
Arts Council, 83
Asian Americans. *See also* Chinese; Japanese
    city offices occupied by, 112
    median household income, 13
    state offices occupied by, 30
    voters, 28
Asians. *See also* Chinese; Japanese
    Americans. *See* Asian Americans
    immigration of, 8, 12
Assembly, 56–57. *See also* Legislature
    speaker of, 56
    Ways and Means Committee, 95
Association of Bay Area Governments (ABAG), 116
Association of Southern California Governments
    (ASCG), 116
"Astroturf" organizations, 46
At-large elections, 111
Attorney general, 87, 88–89
Attorney representation, 71
Auditor of state, 59

Ballot propositions, 23–25, 27. *See also specific*
    proposition
Ballots
    absentee, 28
    party column ballot, 16
    placing candidates on, 17
    split-ticket voting, 16
    typical, 27
Banks, taxation of, 99–100, 101
Baxter, Leone, 32

Bicameral legislature, 52
The Big Five, 96
Bilingual education, 86, 102
Bill of Rights
    Constitution of 1849, 2
    "The Victims' Bill of Rights," 77, 105
Bills into laws. *See* Legislation, passage of
Bird, Rose, 70, 73, 74, 77
Blanket primary, 18
"Blighted" community redevelopment, 115
Board of Equalization, 87, 90
Boards, state, 83
Bond initiatives, 23
Bond revenues, 23
Boxer, Barbara, 123
Brown, Edmund G. "Pat," 7, 88
Brown, Jerry, Jr., 7
    judicial appointments of, 69–70, 73, 74
    vetoes and overrides, 82
Brown, Kathleen, 83
Brown, Willie, 29, 57, 112
Budget
    balancing of, 105
    deficit 2002, 12
    director of finance, 81, 95
    expenditures. *See* Expenditures
    gubernatorial powers/responsibilities, 81, 82, 95
    judicial involvement, 96–97
    legislative participation, 82, 95–96
    process, 94–97
    public participation, 96
    revenue and taxation. *See* Revenue sources;
        Taxation
Bureaucracy of state, 91–92
Burton, John, 58, 64
Business improvement districts (BIDs), 115
Bustamante, Cruz, 29, 57, 88

CalFed, 129
California Abortion Rights Action League (CARAL),
    44
California Association of Realtors (CAR), 42, 43
California Bankers Association, 42
California Business Alliance, 42
California Chamber of Commerce, 42
California Coastal Commissions (CCC), 83
California Correctional Peace Officers Association,
    43, 48
California Council for Environmental and Economic
    Balance, 42
California Democratic Council, 16
California Energy Commission (CEC), 83
California Federation of Labor, 43
California Manufacturers and Technology
    Association, 42
California Medical Association (CMA), 42, 43
California Occupational Safety and Health
    Commission (Cal-OSHA), 83

California Republican Assembly, 16
California School Boards Association, 44–45
California State Association of Counties (CSAC), 45
California State Employees Association (CSEA), 42–43
California State University system, 104
California Teachers Association (CTA), 42
Campaign financing, 25, 31–35, 38
Campaigns, 30–31, 38
Campaign spending
    local elections, 112
    state elections, 31
Campaign support, 47–48
Candidates, 29–30
    ballots, placing on, 17
    financing, 25, 31–35, 38
    preprimary endorsements, 16, 19–20
Capital punishment, 77
Cedillo, Gil, 35
Central committee(s), 18–19
Central Valley growth, 13
Charter cities, 110–111
Charter counties, 109
"Charter schools," 102
Chavez, Cesar, 9
Checchi, Al, 29
Chief Justice, 72–73
Child labor laws, under the Progressives, 5
Chinese
    employment discrimination, 4
    immigrants, 2, 3
    land ownership, 4
    manufacturing jobs, 4
    railroad construction, 3
Cigarette tax, 24, 97, 100, 101
Cities, 109–111. *See also* Local government
    annexation powers, 109
    charter, 110–111
    consolidation, 110
    council–manager system, 112, 113
    councils. *See* City councils
    executive power, 112–113
    expenditures, 119
    general-law, 110, 111
    incorporation of, 109
    mayors, 113
    nonpartisan elections, 5
    revenue and taxation, 118–120
    sales tax, 118
    secession of, 110
    services, charges for, 118
    utility taxes, 118
City council–manager system, 112, 113
City councils, 110, 111
    elections, 111–112
City managers, 110, 112
Civil cases, 70, 71
Civil service system
    creation of, 5
    today, 83
Clinton, Bill, 8, 131–132
Closed primary system, 17–18
College expenditures, 103–104
"Collegiality" among justices, 72
Colonization of California, 2
Colored Convention, 43
Commission on Aging, 83
Commission on Judicial Appointments, 69
Commission on Judicial Performance, 70
Commissions, state, 83
Common Cause, 44
Common interest developments (CIDs), 115
Community-controlled educational centers, 102
Computer-related jobs, 10–11
Conference committee, 60–61
Connell, Kathleen, 97
Conservation programs, under the Progressives, 5

Constitution of California, 73
    of 1849, 2, 52
    of 1879, 4, 52
    amendment of, 8, 23, 59. *See also* Legislation,
        passage of
    right to jury trial, 70
Consultants, political, 24
Consumer Attorneys of California (CAC), 41, 42, 43
Contract lobbyists, 46
Controller, 87, 90
Corporations, taxation of, 99–100, 101
Cost of housing, 13
Councils of government (COGs), 116
Counties, 107–109. *See also* Local government
    board of supervisors, 108
    central committee(s), 18–19
    charter, 109
    courts, 66–67
    executive power, 108
    expenditures, 118, 119, 120
    general-law, 108
    nonpartisan elections, 5
    revenue and taxation, 118–120
    sales tax, 118
    services, charges for, 120
Courts, 66. *See also* Judges and justices
    administration of, 72–73
    budgetary decisions, 96–97
    counties, 66–67
    Courts of Appeal. *See* Courts of Appeal
    and crime, the politics of, 77–78
    2000–2001 litigation, 70
    as political battleground, 73, 78
    Supreme Court. *See* Supreme Court
    trial, 66, 67, 68
Courts of Appeal, 67, 68
    appeals to, 68, 71–72
    initiation of cases, 72
    judges, 69
    "original proceedings," 71–72
Criminal cases, 70, 71
    capital punishment, 77
    plea bargaining, 70
    "The Victims' Bill of Rights," 77, 105
    "three strikes" law, 77–78, 105
Crocker, Charles, 3
Cross-filing, 4–5, 7, 16
Cultural diversity, 8, 12
    in the judicial system, 71
    in the legislature, 54

Davis, Gray, 7, 80–81
    campaign financing of, 32, 43, 47–48
    changes effectuated by, 92
    and the energy crisis, 11, 86–87
    and gun control laws, 78
    judicial appointments of, 74, 75, 86
    legislative special sessions, calling of, 83
    local school bonds and, 24
    spending increase under, 101
    state park fees reduction, 100
    television ads, 34
    vetoes by, 82
Defense-related jobs, 10
Demographic groups, 43
Departments of the state, 84–85
Deukmejian, George, 7, 88
    changes effectuated by, 92
    judicial appointments of, 74, 75
    political popularity and agenda, 86
    vetoes by, 82
de Young brothers, 35
Direct democracy, 21–26. *See also* Initiatives; Recalls;
    Referenda
    ballot propositions, 23–25, 27. *See also specific*
        proposition

Direct democracy *(continued)*
  and interest groups, 49
  introduction of, 5, 16
  in local politics, 116–117
Direct mail campaigning, 33, 34
Director of finance, 81, 95
Discrimination, 127. *See also* Affirmative action;
    Cultural diversity; Minorities; Women
District attorneys, 71
District elections, 111, 112
Diversity. *See* Cultural diversity
Door-to-door campaigns, 35
"Dot-com" businesses, 10, 11
Draper, Tim, 24
Dust Bowl immigration, 5

Economic groups, 41–42
Economy, 8–13
Education. *See* Public education
E-mail campaigns, 34
Endorsements, preprimary, 16, 19–20
End Poverty in California (EPIC) movement, 6
Energy crisis, 11, 83, 86–87
Entertainment industry, 11
Environmental Protection Agency (EPA), 128
Environmental regulation, 9
  air pollution, 127–129
  federal–state relations, 122, 127–129
Ethnic groups. *See* Cultural diversity; Minorities
Executive branch
  attorney general, 87, 88–89
  Board of Equalization, 87, 90
  bureaucracy of, 91–92
  controller, 87, 90
  director of finance, 81, 95
  governor. *See* Governor
  insurance commissioner, 87, 90–91
  interaction and integration of, 92
  lieutenant governor, 87, 88
  secretary of state, 87, 89
  superintendent of public education, 87, 89–90
  treasurer, 87, 90
Expenditures, 101–102
  health and human services programs, 104
  independent expenditures, 32
  limitations on, propositions for, 96, 101
  local government, 119, 120
  prisons, 104–105
  public education, 101–104
  of state, 96, 97

Fair Political Practices Commission (FPPC), 50
Farm corporations. *See* Agribusiness
Federal aids or programs, 122, 130
  in the Bush years, 132
  in the Clinton years, 131–132
Federalism, 130
Federal revenue, 130, 131
Federal–state relations, 122–123
  affirmative action and discrimination, 127
  air pollution, 127–129
  changed rules/new directions, 131–132
  clout in, 123–124
  immigration and, 125–126
  shared resources, 130, 131
  terrorism and, 124–125
  water disputes, 129
Feinstein, Diane, 123
Film industry, 11
Financing campaigns, 25, 31–35, 38
Fiscal officers, 90
Fong, Matt, 30
Fong Eu, March, 30
"Formula government," 102
Friends of the Earth, 44
Future of politics, 13–14

Garamendi, John, 91
Gasoline tax, 97, 100
Gays
  interest groups and, 43
  officeholders, 30
General election, 16
General-law cities, 110, 111
General-law counties, 108
General veto, 82
Geographic divisions, 13
George, Ronald, 73, 76
Get-out-the-vote drives, 35
GI forum, 43
"Golden State," 3, 130
Gold rush, 2
Gonzales, Ron, 113
"Good government," 4
Gore, Al, 8
Governor, 80, 81. *See also specific name of governor*
  budgetary powers/responsibilities, 81, 82, 95
  formal powers, 81–86
  informal powers, 86–87
  judicial appointments, 68, 69, 73, 74, 86
  legislative special sessions, calling of, 83
  political popularity and agenda, 86
  veto power, 82
Grange movement, 4
Grassroots campaigns, 35
Great Depression, 5–6
Growth control, 117–118
Gun control laws, 78
Gun Owners of California, 41

Habeas corpus, 72
Hahn, James, 113, 125
Hayakawa, S.I., 30
Health and human services programs
  expenditures, 104
  for immigrants, 76, 86, 126
Hearst, William Randolph, 35
Helmick, D.O. "Spike," 125
Hertzberg, Bob, 56, 57
High-tech jobs, 10–11
Hill, Elizabeth, 95
History of California, 1–8
"Hit pieces," 34
Home ownership, 13
Home-rule charter cities, 110–111
Hopkins, Mark, 3
Household income, median, 13
Howard Jarvis' Taxpayers Association, 44
Human services programs. *See* Health and human
    services programs
Huntington, Collis, 3

Illegal immigration, 8
Immigration, 2, 3, 125–126
  African Americans, 6
  amnesty for illegal aliens, 8
  Dust Bowl, 5
  illegal, 8
  post-WWII, 8
  and the Progressives, 5
  today, 12
  and Workingmen's Party, 4
Income tax, personal, 98–99, 101
Independent expenditures, 32
Initiatives, 22
  budget, 96
  and interest groups, 49
  introduction of, 5, 16
  legislative, 22–23
Insurance commissioner, 87, 90–91
Insurance premium restrictions, 90
Insurance tax, 97

Interest groups, 40
    campaign support, 47–48
    clout and, 50
    demographic groups, 43
    and direct democracy, 49
    economic groups, 41–42
    evolution of, 40–41
    litigation by, 48–49
    lobbying, 45–47
    professional associations, 42–43
    public, 44–45
    regulation of, 49–50
    single-issue groups, 44
    unions, 42–43
Internet-based "dot-com" businesses, 10, 11
Internet campaigning, 33–34
Investigative reporting, 37
IOUs to state workers, 96
Item veto, 82

Japanese
    immigrants, 5
    WWII prison camps, 6
Johnson, Hiram, 4, 49
Jones, Bill, 89
Judges and justices
    appointment of, 68, 69, 73, 74, 86
    Courts of Appeal, 69
    election of, 68
    removal or reprimand, 69–70
    Supreme Court, 69, 72, 73, 74, 75
    trial courts, 68
Judicial Council, 72–73
Judicial system. See Courts; Judges and justices
Jury trials, 70–71
Justices. See Judges and justices

Kahl/Pownall Advocates, 46
Kearney, Denis, 4
Knight, Goodwin, 88

Labor relations, 9
    unions, 42–43
Land ownership
    Chinese immigrants, 4
    early, 2–3
    Japanese immigrants, 5
    Southern Pacific Railroad, 3
    today, 9
Land rush, 2
Land use
    fiscalization of, 118
    growth control, 117–118
Latinos, 12
    city offices occupied by, 112
    media, 37
    median household income, 13
    state offices occupied by, 29
    voters, 28
Laws, making of. See Legislation, passage of
League of California Cities, 44
League of Women Voters, 44
Legal aid societies, 71
Legislation, passage of, 59–60
    formal process, 60–61, 62–63
    informal process, 61, 64
    vetoes and overrides, 82
Legislative analyst, 59, 95
Legislative committees, 45–46
Legislative counsel, 59
Legislative districts, 53
    reapportionment, 53–54
Legislative "initiatives," 22–23
Legislature, 52–53, 64
    assembly. See Assembly
    the Big Five, 96

bills into laws. See Legislation, passage of
budgetary process, 82, 95–96
campaign spending, 31
conference committee, 60–61
cultural diversity of, 54
gubernatorial appointments, 83
majority/minority party, 56–58
new players/new rules, 54–55
professionalism, shift toward, 53
salaries of, 53
senate. See Senate
special sessions, calling of, 83
staffing, 58–59
term limits, 55–56
Lesbians
    interest groups and, 43
    officeholders, 30
Lieutenant governor, 87, 88
Lincoln–Roosevelt League, 4, 35
Litigation
    by interest groups, 48–49
    in years 2000–2001, 70
Lobbying, 45–47
Local agency formation commission (LAFCO), 109
Local government, 107, 114
    cities. See Cities
    counties. See Counties
    direct democracy in, 116–117
    expenditures, 119, 120
    growth control, 117–118
    limits on, 120
    property tax, 7, 74, 76, 96, 100, 115, 118
    redevelopment agencies, 115
    regional governments, 115–116
    revenue and taxation, 96, 98, 100, 118–120
    school districts, 113–114
    special districts, 114–115
Lockyer, Bill, 58, 88
Logrolling, 61
Los Angeles Times, 35, 37
Lottery, state, 23–24
Low, Henry, 91
Lucas, Malcolm, 75

Mail campaigning, 33, 34
Mail votes, 28
Mandamus, 72
Manufacturing jobs
    Chinese immigrants, 4
    today, 10
Mass media. See Media
Mayors, 113
McClathy, James, 35
Media, 35
    paper politics, 35–36, 37, 38
    reporting on California, 37–38
    television politics, 32–33, 34, 36–37
Median household income, 13
Medi-Cal, 104
Metropolitan Water District, 116
Mexican American Legal Defense Fund (MALDEF),
    43, 49
Mexican American Political Association (MAPA), 43
Mexicans
    amnesty for illegal aliens, 8
    deportation during the Great Depression, 5
    "Zoot Suit Riots," 6
Mexican–U.S. war, 2
Minorities. See also Cultural diversity
    affirmative action. See Affirmative action
    African Americans. See African Americans
    Asian Americans. See Asian Americans
    bilingual education, 86, 102
    discrimination against, 127
    during the Great Depression, 5
    interest groups, 43

Minorities *(continued)*
    Japanese. *See* Japanese
    Latinos. *See* Latinos
    Mexicans. *See* Mexicans
    Native Americans, 2, 3, 24
    post-WWII, 8
    right to vote, 2, 4
    today, 12–13
    women. *See* Women
Missions, 2
Money officers, 90
Mothers Against Drunk Driving (MADD), 41
Murphy, Dick, 113

National Immigration Act of 1924, 5
National Organization for Women (NOW), 43
National Rifle Association (NRA), 44
National Women's Political Caucus (NWPC), 43
Native Americans, 2, 3
    casinos on Indian land, 24
Negative ads, 34
Newspaper politics, 35–36, 37, 38
Nonpartisan city and county elections, 5
Northern California, 13

O'Connell, Jack, 89
"Octopus, The," 3
Olson, Culbert, 6
Otis, Harrison Gray, 35

Paper politics, 35–36, 37, 38
Parties. *See* Political parties
Party column ballot, 16
Pelosi, Nancy, 123
Personal income tax, 98–99, 101
Plea bargaining, 70
Political action committees (PACs), 31
Political consultants, 24
Political parties, 15–26
    central committee(s), 18–19
    major, 17, 18, 19, 20
    Progressive movement, 4–5, 15–16
    structure, 17–20
    supporters, 20
    third parties, 17
    weakness of, 25, 30, 31
    Workingmen's Party, 3–4
Political Reform Act of 1974, 31, 49–50
Population growth, 6
Post-WWII politics, 7–8
Poverty, 12
Preprimary endorsements, 16, 19–20
President pro tem, 57–58, 88
Priest, Serrano v., 102
Primary elections, 16
    blanket primary, 18
    closed system, 17–18
    creation of, 4, 16
Prison expenditures, 104–105
Professional associations, 42–43
Progressive movement, 4–5
    and city elections, 111
    legacy of, 15–16
Property tax, 7, 74, 76, 96, 100, 115, 118
Proposition 4 (state expenditure limits), 96, 101
Proposition 5 (casinos on Indian land), 24
Proposition 8 ("The Victims' Bill of Rights"), 77, 105
Proposition 10 (cigarette tax), 24
Proposition 13 (property tax cuts), 7, 74, 76, 96, 100, 115, 118
Proposition 34 (campaign contribution limits), 32
Proposition 39 (local school bonds), 89
Proposition 98 (public education expenditures), 102, 103
Proposition 103 (insurance premium restrictions), 90
Proposition 111 (state expenditure limits), 96, 101

Proposition 140 (term limits), 55, 56, 58
Proposition 172 (state sales tax increase), 96
Proposition 187 (public services for immigrants), 76, 86, 126
Proposition 209 (affirmative action, elimination of), 86, 127
Proposition 218 (local government tax increases), 96
Proposition 227 (bilingual education, restriction of), 86, 102
Protest referenda, 22
Public defenders, 71
Public education
    bilingual education, restriction of, 86, 102
    expenditures. *See* Public education expenditures
    local school bonds, 89
Public education expenditures, 101–102
    colleges and universities, 103–104
    grades K through 12, 102–103
Public interest groups, 44–45
Public relations firms, 24
Public Utilities Commission (PUC), 83
    creation of, 4

Quackenbush, Chuck, 83, 91

Racial minorities. *See* Minorities
Railroads, 3, 4
    and the Progressives, 4–5, 15–16
Ranches, 3
Reagan, Ronald, 7
    vetoes and overrides, 82
Reapportionment, 53–54
Recalls, 21
    and interest groups, 49
    introduction of, 5, 16
Redevelopment agencies, 115
Referenda, 22
    budget, use for, 96
    introduction of, 5, 16
Regional governments, 115–116
Reiner, Rob, 24
Removal of judges, 69–70
Rental property, 13
Reprimand of judges, 69, 70
Revenue sources, 97–98
    bonds, 100
    federal revenue, California as major source of, 130, 131
    local government, 118–120
    state services, 100
    taxes. *See* Taxation
Reynolds v. Sims, 53
Right to jury trial, 70–71
Riordan, Dick, 34
Roberti, David, 58
Roosevelt, Franklin Delano, 6
Rules Committee of the senate, 58
Runoff elections for judges, 68

Sacramento Bee, 35
Sales tax
    local, 118
    state, 96, 98, 101
Samash, Artie, 45
San Francisco Chronicle, 35
San Francisco Examiner, 35
School districts, 113–114
School vouchers, 103
Schwarzenegger, Arnold, 24
"Scrip" for state workers, 96
Secretary of state, 87, 89
Senate, 57–58. *See also* Legislature
    Budget and Fiscal Review Committee, 95
    gubernatorial appointments, approval of, 83
    president of, 57–58, 88
September 11, 2001, 11, 105, 124–125

Serna, Joe, Jr., 113
Serrano v. Priest, 102
Settlement of civil cases, 71
"Shadow government," 73
Shelley, Kevin, 89
Sierra Club, 44
Silicon Valley, 10–11
Silicon Valley Manufacturing Group, 42
Simon, Bill, 34
Sims, Reynolds v., 53
Sinclair, Upton, 6, 32
Single-issue groups, 44
"Sin" taxes, 101
"Smog exchange" program, 128–129
Soros, George, 24
South Coast Area Air Quality Management Board, 116
South Coast Area Air Quality Management District, 128
Southeast Asian immigration, 8, 12
Southern California, 13
Southern Pacific Railroad, 3, 41
Spanish colonization, 2
Speaker of the assembly, 56
Special districts, 114–115
Spencer, Stuart, 20
Spending. *See* Expenditures
Split-ticket voting, 16
"Spoils" system, 83
Stanford, Leland, 3
State auditor, 59
State boards and commissions, 83
State bureaucracy, 91–92
State central committee(s), 18
State departments and agencies, 84–85. *See also* Local government
State–federal relations. *See* Federal–state relations
Statehood, 2
Suffrage, 2, 4, 5
Superintendent of public education, 87, 89–90
Supplemental Security Income (SSI), 104
Supreme Court, 67, 68
    appeals to, 68, 71–72
    Chief Justice, 72–73, 75
    initiation of cases, 72
    Justices, 69, 72, 73, 74, 75
    "original proceedings," 71–72
    as political battleground, 73
    voter-approved laws, rulings against, 76

Taxation, 94, 97–98, 99
    alcohol tax, 97
    banks, 99–100, 101
    Board of Equalization, 87, 90
    cigarette tax, 24, 97, 100, 101
    compared with other states, 100–101
    corporations, 99–100, 101
    fairness in, 105
    gasoline tax, 97, 100
    insurance tax, 97
    local government, 96, 98, 100, 118–120
    local sales tax, 118
    personal income, 98–99, 101
    property tax, 7, 74, 76, 96, 100, 115, 118
    railroads, preference to, 3, 4
    state sales tax, 96, 98, 101
    user taxes, 97, 100, 101
TechNet, 42
Technical jobs, 10–11
Telephone campaigns, 35
Television politics, 32–33, 34, 36–37
Temporary Assistance for Needy Families Program (TANF), 104
Term limits
    legislature, 55–56, 58
    local officials, 117
Terrorism, 11, 105, 124–125

Third parties, 17
"Three strikes" law, 77–78, 105
Tobacco tax, 24, 97, 100, 101
Tourism industry, 11
Toward Utility Rate Normalization, 44
Transit districts, 116
Treasurer, 87, 90
Trial courts, 66, 67
    judges, 68

Unemployment, 2002, 12
Unions, 42–43
United Farm Workers (UFW), 9, 43
University expenditures, 103–104
University of California, 104
U.S. Congressional clout, 8, 123–124
USA Patriot Act, 124
User taxes, 97, 100, 101
Utility taxes, 118

Van de Kaml, John, 89
Veto power, 82
"Victims' Bill of Rights, The," 77, 105
Villaraigosa, Antonio, 57, 64
Vote. *See also* Ballots
    failure to, 27, 28
    mail votes, 28
    right to, 2, 4, 5
Voter registration, 17, 27
    during gubernatorial election years, 18, 19
Voters, 27–28
    registration of. *See* Voter registration
    and the Supreme Court's independence, 76
Vouchers, 103

Warren, Earl, 7, 88, 89
Water
    federal–state relations, 129
    supply, 9–10, 129
Water projects
    post-WWII, 7
    during the 1930s, 6
Web site campaigning, 33–34
Welfare costs, 104
Wesson, Herb, 29, 57
Westly, Steve, 90
Whitaker, Clem, 32
Wilson, Pete, 7, 81
    affirmative action under, 127
    ballet propositions, use of, 86
    budget battles of, 86, 87–88, 96–97, 101
    changes effectuated by, 92
    and immigration, 8, 24
    judicial appointments of, 74, 75, 86
    personal income tax increase under, 98
    and reapportionment, 54
    sales tax cut by, 98
    and State Finance Commission funding, 83
    vetoes by, 82
    and welfare costs reduction, 104
Wine Institute, 42
Women
    city offices occupied by, 112
    political candidates, 30
    right to vote, 2, 5
Workers' compensation laws, under the Progressives, 5
Workingmen's Party, 3–4
World War II, 6–7
    postwar politics, 7–8
Writs
    of habeas corpus, 72
    of mandamus, 72

"Zoot Suit Riots," 6